FROM RED TO
READ

FROM RED TO
READ

ALAN TONGE

With Michael Garvey   Foreword by Norman Whiteside

The Story of Fergie's First Fledgling

First published by Pitch Publishing, 2024

Pitch Publishing
9 Donnington Park,
85 Birdham Road,
Chichester,
West Sussex,
PO20 7AJ
www.pitchpublishing.co.uk
info@pitchpublishing.co.uk

A CIP catalogue record is available for this book
from the British Library.

ISBN 978 1 80150 664 9

Typesetting and origination by Pitch Publishing
Printed and bound in India by Replika Press Pvt. Ltd.

Contents

This book is dedicated to the greatest teachers and people I've ever known: my father Kenneth, my mother Pamela, my late twin brother Kev, my sister Jan, my nephew Nathan, my son Sam and my daughter Lauren. Without your examples of love, integrity, honour, humility, courage, resilience, morality, ethics, unconditional support and striving to keep walking in light, my life would be nothing.

Kick-off

Acknowledgements

IT HAS always been an ambition of mine to write a book. I was never really sure what it would be about until I got talking to someone at a Manchester United ex-players' association event. After sharing some pleasantries and answering questions about my journey and achievements so far, an elderly gentleman looked me straight in the eye and said, 'You've got such a unique and interesting tale. You should put a book together.' And here we are!

There are lots of different people to thank in relation to this lifelong ambition being realised. Firstly, my incredible, supportive, beautiful family, who I've dedicated this book to. I love and owe you so much that I wouldn't know where to start. I've been very blessed indeed.

I'd like to thank one of my heroes, Norman Whiteside, for providing the foreword and writing some paragraphs about his own experiences and journey, which was absolutely incredible and meant the world. Alongside Bryan Robson, Norman was a huge role model to me growing up and is one of Manchester United's greatest-ever players. To be able to share a pitch with him was an experience I'll never forget – don't give the ball away!

I'd also like to thank those who have taken time out of their busy schedules to revisit and write down some of their memories: Kevin Miller, Danny Bailey, Jon Brown, Kieran Toal, Mike Pollitt,

Craig Lawton, Simon Andrews, Dave Cooper, Paul McGuinness, Jon Richardson, Gary Rice, John Hodge, Dr Mark Nesti and Dr Robert Morris.

Thank you to Tony Park for providing some stats based on the Manchester United teams I represented, Jim Thomas for taking a gem of a picture at The Cliff and allowing us to use it for the book and also to the Grecian Archive for providing data in relation to my time at Exeter City, which has brought back some memories and proved extremely useful. I'm thankful also to newspapers such as the *Express* and *Echo*, the *News of the World* and the *Manchester Evening News*, which sent my family hard copies of photographs that have remained in my collection for many years.

I'd like to thank all my friends and current academic colleagues whose support and encouragement has been invaluable within differing guises. There are simply too many to mention here, but you know who you are. A huge thank you, however, must go to Dr Gerald Griggs and Dr Mike Walsh at UCFB (University Campus of Football Business) for being so understanding and supportive in the process of me writing my PhD. This was a huge component in me achieving it. Some special recognition must also go to an array of top people from the early days at UCFB. Rachel Potts, Emma Potts, Dr Tom Buck, Chris Boyd, Dr Cece Diaz, David Horrocks, Simon Tansey, Dr Leah Johnstone, Rachel Claxton, Colm Griffith, Tom Wenham, Russ Preston, Mo Seedat, Simon Mitton, Ian Tomlinson, Jono McPhail, Jan Mitchell, Stacy Hughes, Carl Wild, Jez Semple, Neil Scott, Chris Shoop-Worrall, Connor McGillick, Laura Davies, Dean Hughes, Wayne Goodison, Darren Bernstein, Chris Cooper, Dr Noel Dempsey, Matt Graham and Christie Scanlon. Throughout my time knowing you all, you've been amazingly supportive and kind in differing ways and have been there to offer encouragement when striving to do things such as writing a book! I'll never forget that.

A big thank you must go to Victoria Myers for being a wonderful former academic colleague and more importantly an incredible friend. Your support has been amazing! Thank you for believing in me and being there for the ups and the downs.

Thanks so much to Jane at Pitch Publishing for believing in and supporting this project, providing your expert guidance and knowledge throughout. This has been absolutely invaluable. Also, to Ivan Butler, Alex Daley and Duncan Olner for their hard work in the editing and design process.

Last, but by no means least, I'd like to thank the brilliant Michael Garvey for believing in the idea, all the support, countless interviews, meetings in coffee shops, drafting, redrafting and basically putting all this together. You've become a very good friend and without your passion and enthusiasm for the project of writing a book, this simply wouldn't have happened.

'A professional footballer? That's not a proper job.'
Meeting a girlfriend's father for the first time

'Okay, let's pick two teams for a seven-a-side. The lads who have got five GCSEs on one team and the thick c***s like me go on the other.'
Eric Harrison before a training session at Man Utd

'An extra 20 quid a week on your wages? No fucking chance. Close the door on your way out.'
Alex Ferguson during my professional contract negotiations

'We're going to have to move you on, son. It will be tough without you but after having a good discussion with Eric, Nobby and Kiddo, it's been decided we'll give it a go.'
Alex Ferguson on my release from Manchester United

'I want you to do something for me that you've not done for a while, son – play well.'
Alan Ball pre-match

'This is Alan Tonge. He played in the same youth team as Ryan Giggs before their careers went in very different directions.'
A Manchester United supporter introducing me to his mate at an ex-players' association dinner

'It's a shame your mum and dad didn't wait a couple of years; you would have been in that Class of '92 crop.'
A Man Utd supporter at an ex-players' golf day

'At least you've got a really unique record of playing two games in one for Manchester United's senior side. Your first and last.'
A Man Utd supporter on social media

'I hope you're a better player than your dad was.'
Sir Alex Ferguson to my son Sam at an ex-players' event

'I'm not sure there's much demand for having me on the wall with my Exeter City shirt on, son.'
Responding to an inquisitive question from my eight-year-old son Sam about Stan Chow's art in the Hotel Football bar area

Foreword by Norman Whiteside

I REMEMBER playing alongside Alan and the other youngsters on a trip to the Isle of Man with Manchester United reserves when I was coming back from injury. I think we won the game comfortably on a windy day. Mark Bosnich was our goalkeeper and got caught out when one of their players crossed the ball and the wind took it over his head into the back of the net. It was hilarious; I remember being stood on the halfway line sucking my finger and sticking it in the air shouting to him, 'Did you not check which way the wind was blowing, Bozzy?'

Alan was a good lad and as a first-team player you got to know all the apprentices from around The Cliff. You'd see them in the canteen, cleaning boots or around the changing rooms. I could relate to them because I'd been through it myself and still have very fond memories of my own time in the youth set-up.

At 15 I was flying over to Manchester on a Friday, playing for the juniors Saturday morning and then going to watch the first team in the afternoon before flying back to Belfast on the Sunday. It gave me a lot of independence because I was travelling on my own, getting taxis to the airport and finding my way to the digs.

I was part of a good youth team. People talk about the Class of '92 but we got to the FA Youth Cup Final ten years before, narrowly losing out to Watford 7-6 over two legs in a hell of a game of football. Nobody really remembers runners-up but that side included the likes of myself, Mark Hughes, Clayton Blackmore, Graeme Hogg, Billy Garton, Mark Dempsey and Nicky Wood, so most of the lads played for the first team or had decent careers in the Football League.

My first-team debut came at Brighton when I was still 16, coming on for Micky Duxbury for the last 12 minutes after a lot of speculation before the game. We won 1-0 and the funny thing about that was I was only on £16 a week as an apprentice. We got on the coach for the journey home and the lads were asking me what I was going to do with my win bonus, which I knew nothing about but turned out to be £800! I remember thinking, *£800 for 12 minutes, this job will do for me!*

I stayed in the team and we won the next four games so I ended up pocketing £3,200, which they couldn't pay me until my 17th birthday. After that it all happened very quickly. I went to the World Cup in 1982 and scored in both the FA and League Cup finals in 1983.

There were so many highs. When you're a kid everyone dreams of scoring the winning goal in the cup final, which I managed to do against Everton in 1985. I wasn't a prolific goalscorer but I did score important goals, including a few against Liverpool and one in a Manchester derby.

When Alex Ferguson arrived at the club in November 1986 he made it clear that he didn't care for reputations and was going to do things his way. I featured regularly in his first couple of seasons and it took a while for him to get any sort of consistency, but once he got the FA Cup in 1990 under his belt he had the nous and knowledge to build on it. He was also very good at identifying when things needed reshaping and when to change his team. Fair play to him.

I moved on in the summer of 1989. We had a chat and he was great at helping me sort my move to Everton. People think me and Fergie fell out or that I was drinking too much but it couldn't be further from the truth. I still see him all the time and we're good mates. Honestly, he was as good as gold and I ended up earning four times more at Everton than I was on at Old Trafford.

I just about passed my medical and managed one full season where I scored 13 goals from midfield, and then a grand total of 60 minutes the following year. My knee gave up and I remember going in for a tackle where I went one way and it went the other. I was only 26 years old but it was clear that I was finished and would have to retire.

The hardest day was waking up one morning with no training or dressing room to go to. It's a heartbreaking realisation for any player and I just got back into bed, put the quilt over my head and cried my eyes out.

Football had given me some great times and been my life but you have to accept you can't do it anymore, find the inner strength to pick yourself up and move on.

I had to go back to school and do my GCSEs and A-Levels. I found it harder to sit in a class of 15-year-old kids than I did playing football in front of thousands of people, which came naturally. I could feel all the eyes on me and remember being scared to put my hand up in case I got the answer wrong. I got over it but it was difficult at first.

From there I attended Salford University and qualified as a podiatrist. I'd always been interested in the medical side of things, probably because I spent so much time in the physio room! You do pick stuff up, and Jim McGregor at United used to give me homework on all the different muscles in the body.

I worked with football clubs for about 15 years doing gait analysis on young players, looking at how they run and walk. I got on the after-dinner speaking circuit and involved with corporate hospitality at Old Trafford, which I've done for nearly 30 years now, so ever since I retired I've always been around the game. Football never leaves you and I always say it's better to be a 'has-been' than not to have been at all.

Education is so important and I know Alan followed a similar path after being forced to retire from the game at a young age. He's taken it further than I did but I would very much encourage young players coming into football to do their education first. Make sure you do your homework and get your GCSEs because it's a short and often fragile career.

That way you can put all your certificates in your bottom drawer just in case you need them one day. Trust me, I know because I had to do it the hard way …

The First Half

Chapter 1

Everything Starts Somewhere

'WE'D LIKE to sign you, son. We think you've got a chance but it's not going to be easy for you.'

The words that most football-obsessed teenagers dream of hearing.

It's January 1987 and the new manager of Manchester United is sat in his office having tea and toast, about to clinch his first signing. But it's not a decorated player with international experience or even someone who's going to make an instant impact, which was probably needed at that time. It's me. A 14-year-old boy from Bolton …

Football had been a big part of my life for as long as I could remember. My dad was a decent player and had been on the books at Oldham and Bury as a youngster. He often jokes that his football career went downhill when he met my mum!

He's a big United supporter and I was brought up on stories of the Busby Babes and George Best, and even now he'll recall matches he went to in the 1950s and 60s. He was at Old Trafford for Bestie's debut against West Brom and remembers the surprise when the team was read out and he was a late replacement for Ian Moir.

The club has always had a certain mystique and magic about it to me. My earliest conscious memory is us winning the 1977 FA Cup Final against Liverpool at Wembley on a red-hot day back when cup finals were cup finals. As a kid I loved all the build-up, which would start in the morning in the team hotels as they ate breakfast, then there might be snooker matches between legends from both clubs and finally the TV crews would be on the coaches with both teams as they made their way to the stadium.

It was a big thing in our household and was even more special if United were involved. We were a decent cup team in those days and the victory over the Scousers was followed by further wins over Brighton in 1983 and Everton in 1985. It wasn't all plain sailing, though, and I can still clearly recall the heartbreak of 1979, when a late goal from Alan Sunderland sealed a crushing 3-2 defeat to Arsenal after we'd battled back from two goals down, which was also one of the only times I've cried at a football match.

There weren't a lot of live televised matches in those days, usually just the big ones or World Cups, and I can remember rushing home from school to see my hero Bryan Robson score that early goal for England against France in 1982. I avidly collected the Panini stickers like most lads my age and would sit mesmerised in front of the TV watching the top continental players play on the biggest stage – the likes of Michel Platini, Karl-Heinz Rummenigge and even Kenny Dalglish. I'd often pretend to be them, playing in the park or playground at school the next day.

For the most part though, my usual routine would be to listen to the United match on the radio in the kitchen every Saturday afternoon before watching the highlights on *Match of the Day* that evening if my parents let me stay up. I didn't go to my first match until my dad took me to Old Trafford as a present for my ninth birthday in the spring of 1981, for a match against Leeds United.

Garry Birtles had recently signed and was still on his quest to score a goal, something that, unfortunately, only Leeds managed that day with Brian Flynn getting a late winner. It was a surreal feeling watching their fans celebrating in the section below us – what's now the South Stand. I remember the excitement of going and the aura around the place but obviously there wasn't much to cheer about after losing to a big rival, so I came away that day feeling that things could only get better.

As a fan you form an identity or special connection to a club usually at a young age. Mine was United and like most kids I dreamed of playing for them. As a young kid I idolised Gary Bailey and actually remember wanting to be a goalkeeper initially. I used to wear a green V-neck top with a white T-shirt underneath to look like him and loved diving around to make saves. You could say that all the diving helped shape my approach to tackling later on when I moved to play outfield!

My dad built some goals in the garden at home for me, and what was particularly enjoyable about that was there always seemed to be scenarios set up like being 1-0 down to Liverpool in extra time. I'd spend hours pretending to be Stuart 'Pancho' Pearson or recreating Jimmy Greenhoff's diving header in the 1979 FA Cup semi-final.

I'd do the same at Mytham Road playing fields, which were very conveniently located at the top of our street and is a place that holds many fond childhood memories. It had a bowling green on one side, a main road on the other and two full-size pitches at the top. I'd usually get home from school, quickly get changed into my playing-out clothes and rush up to the field, where I'd be until it went dark, with a short break for tea.

We'd often join up with whoever was there, playing five-a-side if there were enough of us and making up all the rules ourselves. It was just about having fun and enjoying yourself. I think most of my technique and identity as a player was derived from free play rather than organised coaching. Sadly, I think that's something a lot of youngsters miss out on these days when they get picked up by academies from a young age, being able to develop that early love for the game with no coaches telling you what to do.

On a Saturday afternoon they used to put the proper nets up about an hour prior to kick-off for the local men's team, which presented a dream opportunity to take penalties and bend balls into the top corner while the blokes who were playing were turning up and getting changed. I'd often stay to watch the match too.

My dad worked long hours for British Gas as a courier delivering post but he'd always have time to take me and my twin brother Kev for a kickabout or to play cricket when he got home, no matter what kind of day he'd had. He was and still is a remarkable man who was an absolute bedrock of support and encouragement for us growing up. He'd meander up the road and the magnetism he had meant that as soon as he set foot on that field kids from the neighbourhood would appear from all angles almost like they were drawn by some hypnotic trance. What would start as me, Kev and my dad would often end up in games of seven-a-side, sometimes more!

Crumpled coats or tracksuit tops would be cast to the floor and it would only finish when we could no longer see, well into the cool serene dusk of the evening. Dad made time for everyone and would never judge or criticise, while allowing anyone to join in regardless of their ability or how the game was flowing. As far back as I can remember, he always invested quality authentic time into me and our family. We always seemed to have a football at a park or somewhere with goalposts, and it was a glorious time in my life. Strong foundations were laid at the top of Mytham Road, with morals, values and character put in place.

It was the same at home, where I, along with Kev and our younger sister Janine, benefitted from a strong family environment. My mum is a really top person and a good foil for my dad in a lot of ways. They got married all the way back in 1969 and they're still going strong. She worked quite a few jobs in places such as Hampsons, Thorntons the chocolate shop, on the tills in a supermarket and was a doctor's receptionist for a while, all to bring in some extra income. She always made sure we were sent to school in nice, ironed uniforms, which a lot of kids don't get unfortunately. I wouldn't say she was a lover of football but she'd come and watch to support me or my dad, depending on who was playing.

It was a stable environment and I have a lot to be thankful to my parents for. My nana came to live with us too after my grandad died. She was a beautiful person who lived until she was 97 and would often make me something to eat when I popped home from school for my dinner. There was no materialism, just a lot of love and support that didn't cost anything, with our lives revolving around spending time together. They were all good people and I was very lucky because it gave me the best start in life.

I could sense that I was quite a decent footballer and maybe stood out a bit in my peer group at school. I started playing at grassroots level when I was nine or ten for Farnworth Boys and was there for a couple of years before moving to a club called Moss Bank, which was affiliated to the Bolton town team.

At the age of about 14 a few of us progressed to Bolton Lads Club, which was my first real introduction to a proper coaching set-up. Tony Moulden and Billy Howarth were our coaches. Billy's son Lee was at Blackpool and Tony's lad Paul was absolutely prolific at youth level, famously scoring 340 goals in a single season before being snapped up by Manchester City. I remember us going on a trip to Maine Road to watch him play for City's first team and he'd sometimes come down to training with Lee to help coach us.

I loved playing for Tony and Billy, who were both great coaches, arguably the best I had on my football journey, and I learned a lot from them, which I took forward into later life. They put a lot of faith in me and understood that if you treat someone well, delivering praise at the right times, you can get more out of them. They knew what it took to make it because they both had sons in the game. The training was intense and I remember a lot of cross-country runs around Queens Park in Bolton or fierce two vs twos in the small gym. We had a great team and quite a big rivalry with Horwich RMI, who had also managed to attract some of the best talent in the area. It would be between us and them for who would win the league every year and the results in those fixtures would usually define our season.

Seven of us from the Lads Club went on to serve apprenticeships with Football League clubs with me, Mike Pollitt, Jason Lydiate and Paul Sixsmith all ending up at United together. Neil Hart went to Bolton, our centre-forward Sean Whorlow ended up at Burnley, as did Neil Howarth, who made a few hundred career appearances for the likes of Macclesfield and Cheltenham Town, while Lee Mason became a Premier League referee.

I played for the Bolton Boys Federation Inter League team too where my team-mates included future England cricketer Ronnie Irani, and Garry Flitcroft, who of course went on to play for

Manchester City and Blackburn Rovers. I also made the Greater Manchester County team, so it worked out at one point that I was playing football six days a week! Maybe that was detrimental to me in the long run but I loved it and just wanted to play as much as I could.

A few clubs began to show an interest and I was actually on the radar of my local club Bolton Wanderers from the age of ten or eleven. I remember catching two buses a couple of times a week to go and train in the indoor gym behind their old ground at Burnden Park. There were goals painted on the walls and an outdoor shale surface with a couple of five-a-side nets at each end. Most of the lads from Bolton Boys were training there and the club physio Peter Nightingale used to take us.

I remember playing in a couple of junior tournaments for them and they wanted me to sign schoolboy forms. The Liverpool legend Phil Neal was the manager and I remember him phoning my mum and dad but I didn't want to rush into anything. I just wanted to play football for anyone and everyone and not be tied down.

Despite being from a red household I did briefly flirt with the blue side of Manchester. My maths teacher at school, Mr Mullender, also served as City's scout for the Bolton area and was always sure to let me know of their interest. I remember going to their old training ground at Platt Lane on a couple of occasions and had a very good trial there, scoring in one match we played from a cross that was fizzed in and I just connected with it really well before watching it fly into the top corner.

They also wanted to sign me and I remember being in manager Billy McNeill's office at Maine Road. They had a decent youth set-up with quite a few lads progressing into the first team, such as Paul Lake, Andy Hinchcliffe, Steve Redmond, Ian Brightwell and David White, who all came through in the same crop, but I sort of knew it wasn't for me because I just didn't have any affinity with the club.

I knew I was a reasonable player so decided to hang fire. The advice I was getting from my coaches was not to commit and to keep my options open, because if you signed schoolboy forms with a club you were tied to them until the age of 16. Perhaps it was a subconscious thing too on my part, in the hope that my dreams would come true if United came calling.

Sure enough they did. I was spotted by a scout called George Knight, who covered the Bolton area for United and had been a player for Burnley just after the Second World War. They invited me down to the school of excellence where we trained at The Cliff on a Monday and Thursday night. I used to get the number 94 bus from the top of our road all the way into Manchester and it would drop me round the corner, which was handy.

You'd go into the main building and there would be a couple of physio beds in the middle of the changing room, but I only ever saw them used for dumping loads of kit on. Yellow shirts, dark blue shorts with numbers on and the traditional United socks that were red, white and black. You'd take your pick of what was there and wander over to the indoor AstroTurf feeling ten foot tall because you were kitted out ready for training with Manchester United. You could sense the history and what it meant; it was quite a big thing really. We'd train for about an hour on the AstroTurf. It was always freezing in there and usually felt colder than it was outside. You could see your breath in front of your face.

It was on one of my first trips down there that I met Eric Harrison for the first time. He was wearing his big United coat with his initials on and didn't waste time with any small talk. 'Who's sent you down?' he asked in a gruff manner.

I remember replying quite meekly, 'Erm, George Knight from Bolton.'

It was quite a cold exchange. A few seconds into the circle work we were doing as part of the session he was on to me, telling me to get my touch sorted and my head up when looking for a pass. It was a level above what I'd been used to.

We'd be put through passing drills and it was so demanding. Brian Kidd would take us out for a long-distance run near the old Cussons soap factory and then, when we got back, Eric would pair you up to take part in a 'one-v-one'. This involved playing an eight-a-side match but you'd be directly responsible for one of the opposition. If they broke away from you and scored or your team lost, you'd have to do a forfeit. They were testing our courage and will even then at 14, because you might be absolutely shattered after the run but then you've got to chase someone man for man and beat them. It was brutal; we were like football gladiators and it was very unforgiving.

Things were about to turn up another notch too. On 6 November 1986 I was there for training. We'd just started the session when the new manager Alex Ferguson came in and introduced himself to all the parents and lads who were there. He didn't give a massive speech or anything like that. He just told us to enjoy ourselves but, when you look back at it, it's quite interesting because it was his first day and he'd have been holding the scarf on the Old Trafford pitch earlier on. Now he'd come to The Cliff in the evening to look at all the youngsters who were just schoolboys, eager to get a grip on every aspect of the club from top to bottom. I didn't really know who he was or what he'd achieved up at Aberdeen but it said a lot that the new first-team manager was taking an interest in us.

Not long after I was invited to an extended trial over Christmas and New Year. I'd played in a Greater Manchester County match at Macclesfield's Moss Rose ground against Cheshire, and Joe Brown, who was United's youth development officer, spoke to my parents afterwards and invited me down for a week. I remember he said to them that I could cross a ball really well, which in his opinion not many lads my age could do.

The extended trial started on 28 December so I was staying in the halls of residence at Salford University over the New Year. We trained, played in a couple of practice matches, went to watch a first-team match and the club took us to the cinema on Salford Quays to see Clint Eastwood's latest film *Heartbreak Ridge*.

I think it was the first big trial Fergie held since taking over and there were a lot of lads there from all over the UK. There were quite a few scouts and coaches there too, casting their eyes over the young prospects. Being a United fan from a young age, I remember seeing Sir Matt Busby and Jimmy Murphy observing, so we were also in the presence of absolute footballing royalty.

I had a cracking trial and everything went really well. I was just focused on doing my best, knowing I had nothing to lose. Obviously there was scrutiny but I wasn't really conscious of it. At one point I remember flicking a ball out wide in the match I was playing in and hearing Eric Harrison's approval from the sidelines, which gave me a boost because I knew from training with the club that he didn't praise you often. 'Brilliant, son!'

One morning I was asked to train with the reserves, which was a big deal because I was still only 14 but quite strong for my age, especially in my legs, and had a pretty solid build. I found myself training alongside lads who were a few years older. I hadn't even signed for the club and recall the likes of Mark Robins, Deiniol Graham, Tony Gill, Lee Martin, David Wilson and Russell Beardsmore being in that group.

At the end of the trial it was initially Joe Brown who told me that they were going to offer me something. By that stage I'd spent time training at a few clubs, but once United showed an interest there was only one place I was going to end up. I remember being given a lift back and running down the drive at a hundred miles an hour when I got home to announce to my proud parents that Manchester United wanted to sign me.

I was back at The Cliff on the indoor AstroTurf a few days later when I got the call to go up to see Fergie in the manager's office there. I excitedly walked up the stairs and knocked on the door. My mum and dad were already sat there, and Fergie was behind his desk eating toast. He was deep in conversation with my mum, who's from Dundee, so they already had something in common with the Scottish connection. He was commenting on the lack of playing fields being in use up there and how things had changed since he was young. This was still in the height of Scotland producing a lot of top players but maybe he could see the decline that followed coming.

'Turn round Alan, yeah you've got good lines on your legs. Aye, you've got good lines, son.'

I didn't even know what that meant but it sounded positive and he must have just been weighing me up. He told me this was the first step on the ladder and that it was going to be tough but it would be down to me because they thought I had a chance of making it. He offered me schoolboy terms and a two-year YTS

31

deal when I left school and that was it. There was no fanfare; I just went down the stairs and back into training.

It's more impressive from a personal perspective now looking back at it than when you're going through it as a youngster. I was probably more focused on sorting my PE kit for school the next day and doing my homework when I got home that night. My mum and dad probably saw it as a fantastic opportunity and I was happy about it but it didn't really mean too much at that moment. I was probably quite matter-of-fact about it with my schoolmates the next morning.

But on 13 January 1987 I was confirmed as Alex Ferguson's first-ever acquisition at Manchester United. It's a claim to fame, even if Viv Anderson is more commonly remembered as Fergie's first signing but his transfer from Arsenal didn't happen until the summer. If we're going to split hairs then he can have the accolade of being the first signing the gaffer bought, but technically I was his first-ever non-fee signing!

A few other lads from the Bolton or Greater Manchester area were all signed around the same time – Mike Pollitt, Paul Sixsmith, Jason Lydiate, Chris Taylor and Kieran Toal – the first bits of mortar in the mansion the manager was going to construct.

I've still got the newspaper clipping where it was announced that United were taking us on. My name is spelled as 'Tongue' though, something that was to dog me throughout my life. There was also a quote from the manager which read: 'The youth players bring a special ingredient to the club.'

Fergie was just beginning the process of overhauling the youth system. I remember at the end of his first season there were a lot of shocked and disgruntled parents when none of the under-16s group from the year above us were taken on as apprentices. Ashley Ward was in that group and went on to play for Manchester City and Norwich, and there were a few other decent players in there. Maybe it was a clean sweep because he associated them with the previous regime or he wanted a higher standard of young player.

When he arrived at the club they only had two scouts for the whole of Greater Manchester and he makes reference in one of his books to the fact they signed several young players from the local area after he took over, knowing they weren't good enough but the club needed to make a statement. He doesn't name us specifically but I think it's my group he's referring to as the sacrificial lambs; what a way to be remembered!

My life didn't really change for the next 18 months until leaving school and joining United full-time. I carried on going down to The Cliff for training a couple of nights a week but could still play on Sunday mornings for Bolton Lads Club, which probably helped keep my feet on the ground. It was different back then and sadly youngsters these days are often prevented from playing grassroots football as soon as they get snapped up by academies.

When you're that age football becomes a strong part of your identity but, unlike a lot of lads in the same position, I didn't take my foot off the pedal with my education. Maybe part of me knew that I might need something to fall back on one day, and I was a bright lad. I did well in my exams and came away with a handful of GCSEs. I was reasonably intelligent, even if I didn't know it at the time.

Maybe I wasn't 100 per cent obsessed with football, not in a rebellious way through drinking or anything like that, but because I engaged with other things too. I liked reading and enjoyed other sports such as cricket, golf and tennis, and I loved playing badminton but United put a stop to that when the physio Jim McGregor observed that my calves were rock solid from being on my toes all the time. They told me I'd have problems as I got older and advised that I stopped and concentrated on trying to make a career in football.

On a Saturday morning I'd play for United's 'B' team, which was effectively the fourth team. The 'B' team would usually be the junior players or lads under the age of 18 but you'd occasionally find yourself up against older pros who were maybe coming back from injury and I loved it.

It was a great opportunity and the first step on the path to fulfilling my dream. Sadly my school didn't quite share my enthusiasm and were a bit of a pain when it came to releasing me to play for United on a Saturday morning. They had the rather old-fashioned attitude that playing for the school team took priority. All the other local lads at United were released straightaway by their schools and sometimes in life you have barriers put in front of you that you shouldn't have to face. It's crazy when you look back at it and that could have been my football career finished straight away.

My mum and dad ended up going in to have it out with the headmaster and my PE teacher and eventually a compromise was reached. I'd continue to play for my school team but play for United on alternate Saturdays. Not ideal, but better than nothing.

It wasn't a great start and looking back they should have been more supportive, even if times have changed, because it probably wouldn't happen now. What I took from that is that as a teacher you should nurture and encourage students' ability or opportunity when it becomes apparent, because you have no right to try to stand in someone's way and suppress it. It was a valuable lesson considering the direction my life ended up taking to endeavour to have a positive impact on the lives of young people.

The same can't be said for the impact my PE teacher had on mine, as he wasn't the most supportive and was a bit like the guy from *Kes*. I remember him standing on the touchline during our school matches making comments like: 'Are you going to get into the game today?' 'Should I bring a chair on for you?' It can have quite an effect at a young age mentally when you don't feel that somebody is fully behind you or bothering to try to forge a connection. It sticks with you.

I do have him to thank for switching me to the position where I ended up playing a lot of professional football, although it probably wasn't intentional. I was a central midfielder when I was younger, one who could play a bit but he put me at right-back for a couple of matches with Bolton Schoolboys and that's where I was playing when I was scouted by United.

I was beginning to progress as a player with United but was learning that was a tough school too. At the age of 15 I was picked to play in the second leg of the 'prestigious' Lancashire League Supplementary Cup Final against Crewe at Gresty Road, which was an eye-opening experience and still sticks strongly in my memory, maybe more for the bollocking I got afterwards from Eric Harrison.

It was an under-18s competition but there must have been some injuries ahead of the match and I remember thinking beforehand, *I'm not sure if I'm ready for this.*

The match was played on a Thursday night. It wasn't the best of pitches and everything felt like it was happening at a hundred miles an hour. You'd take a touch and their lads would be on you, and it was a level up from the standard I was used to. I was playing with and against lads that were two or three years older, which is a big thing at that age. I've got a team picture somewhere and the size difference between me and the other lads who had all filled out and developed a bit more is very noticeable.

We won the match and the cup 6-3 on aggregate but for some reason Eric gave me the full-blown hairdryer treatment in the dressing room afterwards. It was unbelievable and not a nice thing at all to experience. I hadn't even started at the club full-time but was on the receiving end of a verbal assault that basically ended with: 'YOU'VE BEEN ABSOLUTELY FUCKING USELESS TONIGHT!!!'

It was a nasty vitriolic tirade that I totally wasn't expecting and a real shock to the system because I hadn't a clue what I'd done so wrong. I'd had cross words and sly jibes off other coaches previously but this was on another level entirely. I was only 15 years old and was still a child really so hadn't the means in me to say anything or fight back. I had no choice but to sit there and take it. I honestly didn't know what to say to my mum and dad afterwards and just sat in relative silence during the car journey home. It was a really strange feeling.

I reflect on this experience now in my later years and having been in education for a long time as my second career. It was tantamount to the great racehorse trainers Aidan O' Brien, Henry Cecil or John Gosden telling the jockey to whip the life out of a two-year-old on its first run. You simply don't do that. Nurture it, show it and educate it. I was a young footballer doing my best playing three years up in an under-18s team. I respected Eric but he got it totally wrong on that occasion.

I think one of the worst things in football (and life) is being belittled in front of other players (or people), especially in a tight dressing room. It can cause a lot of shit in your head because it's hard to deal with and you don't know how to react, especially at that tender age.

I remember I was playing in the 'B' team on the following Saturday morning. Heading into The Cliff to get some stuff, Eric pulled me on the stairs and apologised: 'I'm sorry, son. I was out of order on Thursday night. I shouldn't have spoken to you like that. It's for your own good though.'

I appreciated the apology but it still left a mark on me, a deep scar that created doubts in my own confidence and ability, leading to overthinking and anxiety issues. It definitely closed me up a bit.

Welcome to the world of professional football!

Chapter 2

The Best of Times, the Worst of Times

THE LIFE of an apprentice at Manchester United in the late 1980s was anything but glamorous or even the football education I'd hoped it would be. I was back on the 94 bus at half six in the morning for the 45-minute journey to The Cliff and still recall my first day vividly, although not for the right reasons.

It was the start of pre-season during the summer of 1988 and most of the lads were unsure of the appropriate attire to turn up in, so there were a few dressed in suits, which quickly changed to tracksuits over the following days. We got changed and went out to train, which inevitably involved a lot of running, but when we got back into the changing room I realised my watch, which had been a present, was missing. It had been nicked, and although the club did deal with the situation by giving me the money for a replacement, it rattled me a bit. When something like that happens it can be hard to trust the people around you, especially in a new environment, so it wasn't a great start.

The apprenticeship wasn't an easy gig by any means. The days were long – sometimes we didn't leave until after 5pm – and the wages at £28.50 a week rising to a princely £35 in our second year were meagre. I was also entitled to a small travel allowance, which amounted to an extra £6 a week to cover all those trips on the 94, but it still equated to a pittance if you broke it down as an hourly rate.

We didn't just train and play football. We were expected to perform menial tasks around the club to help with the upkeep of the place. Every apprentice was given a different role, which changed every so often – you could be working in the ticket office at Old Trafford or helping the groundsman with the pitch. Often you'd find yourself at The Cliff pumping balls up, sweeping the dressing rooms and cleaning the showers, or collecting kit in to be washed. I had to clean the gym. I'd tidy everything, sweep it and mop it once a week on a Friday. All the weights and benches would need cleaning and when you'd finished your handiwork would be inspected by our youth-team coach Eric Harrison. If it wasn't up to standard, he'd say, 'Sort that out, I'll be back down in another half-hour.' It was like being in the military and he wouldn't let you go home until he was happy with everything. There was probably a bit of mind games too, because he'd often go back upstairs to his office for at least another 45 minutes before coming down to check again.

It could be tedious and mundane but it taught values and kept you humble. It was hard work but everyone would muck in together and it gave us a sense of responsibility. I don't think a little bit of that would harm young players coming through these days because everything just seems so easy for them, which can lead to a sense of entitlement.

One of the more enjoyable jobs was cleaning boots. I used to clean Gary Walsh's and you'd get two or three pairs each to do in the old boot room at The Cliff, which had loads of pigeonholes and smelt of dubbin. I loved it because all my heroes' boots were in there – Bryan Robson's pair of New Balance and all the other first-team players, such as Norman Whiteside, Gordon Strachan and Paul McGrath. It was a surreal moment the first time I saw my own pigeonhole labelled 'A. Tonge' alongside them. You'd have to get all the grass off and wipe the boots down before cleaning and polishing them. It was a big part of the culture and was quite satisfying in a way. You'd sometimes get a tip of £10, or £20 usually at Christmas, which was a lot of money to us. Almost doubling our wages!

Sometimes we'd have to do them after the first-team match at Old Trafford, where you'd just get the grass and mud off before they went back to The Cliff for polishing. We'd be milling about in the corridors before the match and would often be there to see the away team arrive. I remember seeing Paul Gascoigne when Spurs were the visitors, in his tracksuit, and he had a little ball in his hand that he was messing about with, but the guy just oozed confidence. When United played Nottingham Forest, Brian Clough gave one of us a pair of shoes with instructions to go away and clean before returning them to the away dressing room.

When the match started we'd sit right behind the dugout and, as an aspiring young full-back, it was a perfect vantage point to study some of the best in the business – the likes of Liverpool's Steve Nicol, Arsenal's Lee Dixon, Brian Laws of Nottingham Forest and Mel Sterland at Leeds United. I'd sometimes have a discussion with Eric Harrison afterwards about their strengths and maybe how I could incorporate some of them into my own game.

We'd watch the match and walk back up the tunnel afterwards, which really made you feel like you were part of it. I used to allow myself to imagine that one day it could be me walking off that pitch alongside my heroes Robbo and Whiteside. It could be pretty awkward if the match hadn't gone well though, because we'd have to stand in the corridor outside the dressing room listening to the gaffer ranting and raving for ages, waiting for the boots to come out for cleaning.

The jobs were tough but, like I say, none of it did us any harm. There was other stuff that went on, though, that was a bit darker and more unpleasant, and in fairness probably wasn't exclusive to United or even football clubs at the time. There were quite a few surprises that lurked around corners and a lot of the second-year apprentices or young pros wouldn't miss an opportunity to assert their seniority over the younger lads. The stories about what went on have been told before but here are a few that I can remember.

There was a medical bed in the middle of the youth-team dressing room and there was a ritual called 'shag the bed' where you'd have to get on it, act out foreplay and then show all your moves. As a 16-year-old that was tough in front of a group of fellow adolescents, and a lot of lads who were maybe a bit more introverted like me found it a difficult experience.

There was another game called 'blagging' where someone would come up to you and say that the gaffer wanted to speak to you in his office. Quite a few were caught out by it and would nervously make their way up the stairs before being abruptly told to get lost because Fergie didn't have a clue what they were on about. 'What the fuck are you talking about, son?'

If you hadn't done one of your jobs properly that could lead to you becoming the defendant in a mock trial where the judge and jury were your fellow apprentices. It would then inevitably lead to a guilty verdict and forfeit where you'd have Vaseline smeared in your hair or be pinned down with a ball smashed in your face from close range. You'd often see lads with nasty abrasions on their arms where they'd had dubbin rubbed on them with a wire brush, and that stuff is an absolute nightmare to get off. You'd be scrubbing yourself for hours.

People would be made to climb into tumble dryers in the kit room or be whipped with a towel as they walked past. I remember another apprentice being made to run around naked outside in the snow wearing only assistant manager Archie Knox's bobble hat while getting pelted with snowballs! Some of it was daft or could be classed as banter, like lads being crammed into the sauna to see how many would fit, squirting shampoo in your hair in the showers when you weren't looking so you'd have to wash it again, flicking ears on cold mornings or putting Deep Heat in each other's boxer shorts, but lines were often crossed. To an extent it was character-building for want of a better phrase but there were lads who really struggled with it. I know I did, and when you're on the receiving end it's hard to see the funny side.

It wasn't very mature but to be fair none of us were having left school five minutes ago and when you come in at 16 you don't know any different. Similar things will have happened on factory shop floors and in many other workplaces. Eric Harrison used to turn up on occasion in the doorway of the dressing room when there was something stupid happening. He'd often have a surprised look on his face but would just start laughing or make light of it.

It was an exceptionally tough environment and after a while it starts to conflict with your identity. I'd been brought up with good morals in a decent family and just wanted to get on and do well at United. I was there to try to develop myself as a footballer and hopefully earn a professional contract. Now suddenly I was getting pushed around a bit, but if I didn't want to do something I'd refuse or stand my ground because I could handle myself.

I remember quite a funny incident with Russell Beardsmore where someone I knew had asked me whether I could get a signed ball from all the first team. I nervously walked into their dressing room with my pen and ball in a plastic bag. They all signed it and it looked superb. All the signatures were on there – Robbo, Brucey, Kevin Moran, Gordon Strachan. It was fantastic. I left the ball hung up in the dressing room while I went out to train and Russell must have been injured at the time because he wasn't training. When I got back and looked at the ball in the bag all the signatures had faded because he'd rolled it in the showers. They were pretty much gone and I was absolutely fuming. I remember thinking, *Right you little bastard, how can I get you back for this?*

We used to have to go to Old Trafford once a week to collect our wages from the reception area near where the Munich tunnel is now. You'd go in and there would be loads of pigeonholes with everyone's initials that housed your wages in an envelope and two complimentary tickets for that weekend's match. That week I noticed that Russell's tickets were still in his pigeonhole so I slipped them in my tracksuit pocket to use as leverage, which soon put the wind up him. He was literally on his knees begging: 'Tongey, please, I need those tickets for Saturday.'

'Get my ball signed again and you'll get them.'

I was adamant he wasn't getting them until he'd sorted it, to prove I had enough courage to sort stuff out and wasn't a shrinking violet. To his credit Russell got another ball signed and I gave him his tickets back. I'm still in touch with him now and he's a smashing lad who's very down to earth and humble. It just goes to show how 'banter' in an environment can change you.

There was a lot of toxic masculinity among the young players, which created a bit of a bullying culture. I was lucky in a way because I was still living at home and free to go back to the sanctuary of my parents' house in Bolton when I clocked off for the day, whereas the madness seemed to continue for the lads from outside the Greater Manchester area who were living in digs. It sounded like a bit of a nightmare, and looking back was probably a recipe for disaster to have a load of bored teenagers all living together in the same house with long evenings to fill. I seem to remember Darren Ferguson moving into digs and moving back out not long after.

You'd get lads coming in on a Monday morning proudly telling stories of their sexual conquests or whatever else they'd been up to on the weekend. Discotheque Royale was the place in Manchester at that time and most of the lads were heading there on a Saturday night or maybe to the Hacienda, which was in its prime. I had a steady girlfriend at the time and other hobbies, which suited me because it allowed me to switch off.

My only experience of the digs was that I'd occasionally pop round to one of the houses, which was run by a lady called Brenda Gosling, after training if I had a match in the evening, to save me going all the way home. The place was more affectionately known as 'Brenda's' and was a bit of a free-for-all, with about ten lads all sat round the kitchen table having loads of banter and messing about. Brenda was a nice lady, quite a smiley person, and I'd just have some tea and toast before making my way to the match.

To be honest I was never jealous of the lads who resided there or in the other houses that provided accommodation for young players at the club. It did cause fractures in the group between the local lads who still lived at home and the lads in digs because it meant there were two groups of us that were having very contrasting experiences.

That was also apparent when it came to continuing our education. If you had five GCSEs you were sent to Accrington College to study for a BTEC national in sports studies, while everyone else went to do an NVQ at a college in Manchester. It was pretty obvious that some of the lads saw it as a waste of time and didn't want to be there, because they'd mess about. I enjoyed it though, and got on well with my tutor, a lady called Patricia Keppie, who was very supportive. There were lads from other local clubs in our class and, to be fair, we had some bright lads in our group at United. Kieran Toal was one who was very academic. He's now a major player in the law industry. He was doing A-Levels alongside his apprenticeship, which was rare back then.

In training Eric Harrison would set us up for a five-a-side with 'The Brainboxes' vs 'The Thick Cunts' and you always felt that he favoured the latter because he'd throw in little jibes about it: 'How many GCSEs have you got?'

'I got three As, two Bs ...'

'What the fuck are you doing here, then?'

The whole set-up was worlds apart from what academy players know nowadays and the support they get, where education is better understood and valued. Lads who had a sensitive side to them or weren't as mature would be given a hard time and there was a lot of stuff that went on that could probably be classed as bullying.

I'd hoped it would be more supportive and about developing ourselves as footballers; following in the footsteps of the Busby Babes that I'd heard so many stories about growing up in an elite school of football. The truth was you were living very much in an adult world while still just a kid, which wasn't easy. You had to grow up quickly and a lot of the lads there became institutionalised because it was literally survival of the fittest.

In my mind I was wrestling with myself because probably the hardest thing I found at United was holding on to my values when it would have made my life easier to become one of the crowd. If belittling others or giving people a hard time was the sort of character you needed to be to progress then I knew that wasn't me. At the time the culture within the club was one my values didn't align with and it was a tough and challenging experience.

I believe a few years later, around the time of the Class of '92, one of the parents complained about some of the stuff that was going on and it was stamped out almost overnight. The success followed, probably because it allowed those lads to concentrate on their football without having to worry about what was going to happen when they finished training.

Looking back, I probably showed a lot of courage and mental resilience to dig in but it was hard to enjoy it at times. As a kid you start playing football for the enjoyment, but once you progress into a professional environment with its increased level of harshness and structured training you do lose a little bit of it. I'm sure even nowadays a lot of youngsters probably feel the same way.

I sometimes used to sit on the bus on the way to The Cliff and think to myself, *Is there anything else that I could be doing?* I felt guilty for thinking that and it's quite sad really because it was a great opportunity and most lads my age would have done anything to be in my position. It would have taken a lot of courage to say that it wasn't for me and that I wanted to look for something else. Maybe if I had come along a few years later it would have been different but it just wasn't what I thought it would be.

Admittedly there were good times too, even if they didn't always feel comfortable at the time. At Christmas they'd move all the tables and chairs to one side in The Cliff canteen and the apprentices would have to act out a pantomime or comedy show for the first team and coaching staff. Lads would have to stand on a table and sing a song using a brush for a microphone or do impressions. It was pretty terrifying and got built up for quite a few weeks beforehand. From memory I got away with just telling a joke I'd heard on the TV from Bernard Manning; it took me a little while to get it out because it was nerve-wracking but it got a few laughs from the audience and I remember sitting back down relieved that my moment was over.

In my first year I was part of the 'B' team winning the Lancashire League Division 2, the first United team to do it since 1972, which wasn't bad. We finished 11 points clear of our nearest rivals Tranmere Rovers and won 23 out of 28 fixtures!

My standing among the other apprentices also got a boost when I passed my driving test quite early at about 17 and a half. I got myself a little Ford Fiesta, which brought me on a bit and meant the other lads were always wanting a lift over to Littleton Road from The Cliff or home after training or back from matches. I almost became a personal taxi service for Mark Bosnich, who was one of the main culprits. He'd often say, 'Tongey, my youth team buddy, will you give me a lift back to the digs after the game tonight?'

Bozza was a typical Aussie who was very laid-back. He sometimes struggled with his kicking but was a great shot-stopper and that's what forged him a career. He had the biggest feet I'd ever seen, because his boots must have been size 12. I used to feel sorry for the apprentice who had to clean them because it would have taken half an hour to do each one! He had a great career, not without problems, which to his credit he's turned around, and I'm still in touch with him through social media. A nice fella.

Reminders of the history of Manchester United that I'd been brought up on were all around too, and it was such a thrill to rub shoulders with and learn from people who could only be described as legends. Nobby Stiles and Brian Kidd were both employed by the club as youth-team coaches and would join in with the five-a-sides in training. They could still put it about and I had great respect for them because they'd been there and done it at the highest level.

I loved Nobby in particular because he was a brilliant, humble guy who was United through and through. He was a good judge of a player, once telling me that my left foot was just my 'swinger' and he wasn't wrong, in fairness. I remember getting some unbelievable praise off him after playing well in an FA Youth Cup tie at Old Trafford where we beat Ipswich Town 4-1. We'd gone to Littleton Road the morning after for a light session and I remember him sidling up to tell me that I was 'fucking brilliant' the night before. 'I loved the way you dug in and your determination last night, Tongey. You dealt with everything brilliantly.' To hear that from a World Cup and European Cup winner made me feel ten feet tall. Absolutely amazing.

We had an orange minibus that was used to travel to away fixtures and once dropped Nobby off on the way home. I remember being taken aback by his house. Here was an absolute legend of the game living in a pretty standard house and it hits you that they're just normal people who were by and large on normal wages.

There was an aura around the club that, despite the challenges, made it feel pretty special. You could sense the history and at times see it for yourself. Sir Matt Busby still had an office and would appear on occasion to watch our matches or come on the odd away trip. We'd see the likes of Bobby Charlton and Wilf McGuinness around the place and I remember bumping into George Best on the forecourt at Old Trafford as a few of us were picking up our wages one afternoon. He had a little chat with us and, although I can't remember exactly what was said, I must have rushed home to tell my dad!

You were very aware of what you were representing and it was a great honour, but following in the footsteps of the Busby Babes wasn't an easy task at a club that was still striving to recapture the glories of yesteryear.

Chapter 3

Eric Harrison and His Scraping Sambas

'OKAY, LET'S pick two teams for a seven-a-side. The lads who have got five GCSEs go on one team and the thick c***s like me go on the other.'

Eric Harrison had a way with words and a big impact on my young life. He'd been a professional footballer himself but not at the highest level. His most notable spells had come at Halifax Town and Barrow before moving into coaching, at first with Everton before joining United in the early days of Ron Atkinson, where he'd overseen the development of Mark Hughes and Norman Whiteside, but I think when Fergie came to the club he was a bit disappointed with the youth set-up.

It's been said that United only had two scouts for the whole of Greater Manchester, which is unbelievable really. Fergie was aware of the history of the club and wanted to start bringing young players through again so the scouting system was ripped up and put back together.

United weren't after the best boy in the street but the best in the area. They got a lot of local kids in at first as part of my intake and immediately after, but you sensed that bigger things were coming and Eric would have been under pressure to produce players for the first team. Eric was an interesting character, uncompromising like a sergeant major and a hard taskmaster. There was a genuine fear of him even if he did look a bit like the comedian Norman Collier, which became a running joke at the club. They had the same sort of wavy hair so that was his nickname.

He was the main youth-team coach and took the 'A' team on a Saturday morning once you'd been 'lucky' enough to earn a promotion from the 'B' team with Brian Kidd, which was probably slightly more developmental, if such a thing existed. He used to watch our games at The Cliff from the coaches' room upstairs to give himself an aerial view of the pitch. If somebody gave the ball away or made an error you used to hear him banging on the window, usually followed by a few expletives. It was a miracle the window didn't crash out!

It was a horrible feeling if you were unfortunate enough to make a mistake early on in a match because you'd be dreading half-time and being on the receiving end of the resultant bollocking. You could tell he was angry when you came into the dressing room and he'd be pacing up and down, scraping the studs of his Adidas Sambas on the floor, like a bull!

He was as tough as the gaffer and there was a big fear factor at United, which was largely driven by those two. They were similar characters; I think Fergie was the main man but Eric played up to him. He tended to be more volatile when the manager was around and maybe felt a bit vulnerable at times. Nobby Stiles and Brian Kidd were both there and were European Cup winners. Eric's playing career hadn't been as successful so he probably thought he needed to cement his niche.

In professional sport you need an element of fear but too much of it can have a destructive impact because it stops players expressing themselves. I had a decent passing range and could play a bit. I scored quite a lot of goals in schoolboy football and I could whip crosses in and join attacks but Eric really favoured the defensive side of the game and liked his players to get stuck in, so any attacking intent I felt ended up being suppressed. I was usually deployed at United as a right-back or centre-half and I'd often find myself playing the easy ball during matches simply to avoid getting a tirade from the sidelines or at half-time. I've often heard that 'simplicity is genius' but it sometimes spoils the fun of trying something different or creative, and looking back I definitely played within myself at times.

The methods employed by the coaching staff also pushed me to start doing things that weren't part of my game. I was a decent tackler with good strength but they'd encourage you to go in hard or through players, which Eric called going underneath. Football was still a very physical game in those days with a lot of hard men knocking about, so he wanted his players to be able to deal with that.

It was almost like they were trying to break us down to build back up in their image but it gave me an identity crisis because I felt I had more to offer. I was caught in a void of wanting to express myself and enjoy playing or doing what the coaches wanted to stay in the team and stand a chance of progressing.

There were a lot of mixed messages, too. I got sent off for a bad tackle after losing my head in the FA Youth Cup at Port Vale just a week or two after Eric had told me I needed to get wired in more. One of their lads said something to me a few minutes before so I marked his card, and as I walked past the dugout on my way to the dressing room I heard Eric say, 'You've fucking let this club down.'

Another time we went to a function at Old Trafford and Archie Knox, another character who was feared among the apprentices because he was brash and straight to the point, was trying to make us go on to the dancefloor and take it in turns to do a stupid dance. We were in our club suits and ties and I didn't see the sense in it, so refused when my turn came. It just wasn't who I was and I stood my ground again when he tried to force the issue. The next morning, I got called up to the coaches' office thinking I was in for it. Archie and Eric were both in there and I remember them having some banter with each other across the room and Eric goading Archie by saying, 'Well done, Tongey, for standing up for yourself.' It could quite easily have gone the other way and I could have been running laps of The Cliff with another bollocking ringing in my ears. It was difficult to know where you stood at times.

We were all given a logbook as part of our apprenticeship to track our development. I've still got mine and, flicking through it a while ago, it's full of comments from Eric like: 'Must develop more of a personality, far too quiet.' 'Needs to talk more in games.' 'Communicate more because when you communicate you concentrate.'

I was a bit more reserved than most of the other lads and it was a difficult environment to try to come out of your shell in. I'd describe myself as a strong but silent type. You've obviously got stuff going through your head and it isn't good from a mental health point of view to not express yourself fully but that's how it was. What's interesting is the contrast with my college reports at the time or when I did some work experience in the ticket office at Old Trafford: 'Shows a good personality.' 'Good manners, polite with the public and seems confident in what he's doing.'

I had people skills and basic decency but I think to make it at United they were looking for something more. I was probably a bit too quiet and perhaps the coaches preferred players who had plenty to say for themselves, had a bit of devilment in them or were just daft, which made them stand out. Maybe I was too content at times to be part of the group and blend in. The thing is you can't become someone that you're not, which should be accepted. It's like Einstein's quote around giving a diverse group of animals a climbing task: 'Everyone is a genius, but if you judge a fish by its ability to climb a tree, it will live its whole life believing it is stupid.' At the time, football culture was largely fixed and rigid.

Eric loved the battles in matches and liked his players to show character. He'd be desperate to win whenever we played Liverpool because they were still the dominant force in English football, and also against his former employers Everton. I remember in one match against Liverpool at The Cliff where it kicked off and he was on the touchline shouting, 'Let them fight!'

Those matches were tough and Liverpool always had very good youth teams who had a certain way of playing. They were all about pass and move and I remember they had a little midfielder called Mike Marsh who was a fantastic footballer. We had some decent results against them and a few good wins on their old training ground at Melwood. It's just as well because losing was unacceptable.

It was much the same but for different reasons when we went to play at Marine or Southport. Carlisle United reserves was another one and the two hours in a minibus to get up there was never an attractive proposition. You'd be playing against adults with beards but Eric loved it because it was a test for a bunch of under-18s and he'd be watching to see how you dealt with it.

You can imagine what it was like. A shit pitch with no grass on it, tight and bobbly with long throw-ins being hurled into the box. If Marine came to The Cliff we'd usually beat them quite convincingly because of the difference in quality but they were tight matches when we played at their ground. It was sink or swim and Eric would make sure he got his message across after the match as to how well we'd come through it. He wouldn't hesitate to tell you the truth, which isn't always nice to hear but sometimes you need it. Young players nowadays often struggle to take criticism and coaches fear losing their jobs if they're too hard on them. There's been quite a few reports in recent years of bullying at clubs and it happened in our day but the difference was that you didn't hear about it. Players are very powerful now and a consequence of that is they often don't get told the truth when they really need it most. Eric didn't care, and if you were shit he'd tell you to your face.

It did give you a bit of steel because he basically instilled in us how to be comfortable being uncomfortable, which gave you courage when things weren't going well to fight through it. You needed a lot of bottle to deal with it and a large part of football is about how you react to adversity. If you don't face difficult times how can you ever grow into something, because you're going to shy away or let someone else do it for you? You had to take responsibility and give 100 per cent in everything you did because to him anything less was unforgivable.

He hated players turning their back on the ball. If he caught someone doing it he'd make them hang on the crossbar and he'd half-volley balls at them from the penalty spot so they'd have to block the ball without turning their back. It wouldn't happen these days but Eric was from a tough school and probably had to fight throughout his life for everything he had. With a lot of coaches their own experience in the game influences how they treat their players, like a rite of passage, and he'd often tell us stories: 'You lot don't know you're fucking born. When I was playing non-league for Halifax I had an older pro having me by the scruff of the neck telling me I'd cost him his win bonus.'

I learned for myself later that non-league football is a tough business. He was grounded and wasn't going to let us get carried away just because we were at United. You don't realise it at the time but life is a tough journey and nothing is given to you on a plate. He'd be testing you all the time and nothing got past him. It was about character sometimes because you could have a brilliant match but he'd remember the one time that you gave the ball away early doors. On the rare occasion that he did give praise you'd be buzzing, but I think it was a distinct trait of old-school coaches to rarely give positive feedback. If you got a 'well done' from Eric you knew you were doing alright and would try to make the most of it because it didn't come often. One of the main differences I found when transitioning from grassroots football to United was they expected more of you and the level of scrutiny was intense.

Every match I played for Eric was about winning and that included friendlies. I don't recall playing any fixtures at United that were developmental. We were a winning machine at youth level and when you look at the records of those teams in old yearbooks now they're unbelievable. We won Lancashire leagues and cups season after season, consistently scoring the most goals and conceding very few, so something was working; however, it came at a detriment to some lads' development because of the culture and the way it was achieved.

I remember sitting down with Eric for a one-to-one at the end of a season where I'd been part of the 'A' team that had just won another league title. I felt like I'd had a decent campaign and was beginning to fill out physically, so imagine how deflated I was when he pulled out a list and started to reel off everything I'd done wrong that season, including specific examples of my mistakes!

What struck me coming away from that was the levels required. We'd just won the league but in his eyes there was always room for improvement and often it felt like nothing was ever enough. When we used to win trophies at youth level there was a distinct lack of fanfare. The trophy and medals would arrive in a box and be handed out among everyone involved; we might have a team photo then we'd just move on to whatever was next. It was relentless.

Eric and I had some sort of connection but it was limited. My personality and my background didn't fit what he wanted me to become and our relationship ended up being quite distant. I respected him absolutely and showed that by always giving my all but he was a tough man who was difficult to please. I was a quiet lad who was a decent player and always looked after myself but I found aspects of his approach quite difficult to deal with.

In that environment you can't be affected by stuff and need to become hardened and almost desensitised to what's going on around you, which I struggled with. Some of the lads used to try to suck up to him to get in his good books but that wasn't me either. To get to the top of any organisation you need to make strong connections with important people and trust them but I never really felt that he believed in me like he did with the Class of '92 lads, who all speak very highly of him.

I was the sort of player who needed a bit of praise and encouragement to get the best out of me but I think if you look at the likes of David Beckham and Paul Scholes, who both made it to the top and stayed there for a long time, they didn't need that. They had an inner confidence about them, which was almost self-generated. Chris Casper once told me that Beckham was the most confident, self-assured person he'd ever met. He had the courage to try his 50-yard 'Hollywood' passes in youth-team matches again even after he'd received a bollocking from Eric. I'd have taken the feedback on and just played safe, and maybe that's the difference in getting noticed and going to the next level.

Knowing that the coach believes in you can make a huge difference and even make or break your career. My Bolton Lads Club manager Tony Moulden used to praise me all the time and I absolutely loved playing for him but I didn't really get that with Eric or any of the main stakeholders at United. You were almost wandering round waiting for that connection, which sadly never came for a lot of lads.

I think what Eric instilled in me was the drive to excel, which is important, but my way of achieving that would differ from his and utilise different methods. I work with young people now and I think you have to show support, patience and encouragement to nurture talent. I know with my make-up that's the approach I'd have preferred but never really got.

Sometimes, though, you pick up things from people without realising until later and that was probably the case with Eric. The resilience and courage that he instilled did have a positive impact on me because life isn't an easy pathway and he knew that. His record of bringing players through who did a lot for Manchester United speaks for itself. He's probably one of the greatest youth coaches of all time and I'll always remember him as a tough, old-school, steely mentor who instilled the importance of character and mental fortitude in his players.

There was no compromising with Eric. If he said, you did … very quickly, or else!

Chapter 4

Little Wembley

IT MUST have been quite a sight for the people on the pitch-and-putt or walking their dog in Heaton Park one summer's day in the late 80s to witness a sea of Manchester United players including several internationals and yours truly hurtling towards them. Imagine that these days!

Pre-season at United was always tough and the first team, reserves and youth team would all be together. It wasn't scientifically based at all, just a lot of running! We'd be running up hills or to certain landmarks and back. Not seeing a ball for the first couple of weeks, just cones to run around.

Brian Kidd and Archie Knox often used to lead the runs and hadn't lost their fitness, because they'd often set the pace with us all behind them. Kiddo was a fantastic coach, a bit more developmental than Eric Harrison and he understood players. He was more about encouragement and praise than having a go but could still dish out a bollocking if required.

I remember one of the lads in the year above dared to have a go back at him after a 'B' team match once over at Littleton Road. Boy it went off, and the two of them had to be separated. It was another occasion as a 16-year-old where you sat there watching things unfold, not knowing what to make of it all. At times it was like living on a volcano that was waiting to explode.

Once that initial fortnight or so was out the way we'd start practice matches and you'd begin to get into your groove for the season ahead. Training sessions would usually start with us running two long laps round Littleton Road, where we often trained to get warmed up, then some static stretches. We'd maybe do some sprinting work or 'doggies' where Eric Harrison would match you up in a race with someone of similar speed. Then they'd put us through drills, which would often involve a lot of repetition such as heading and passing work. We'd do 'rondos' in circles with one or two guys in the middle, which hasn't really changed, and practise phases of play where you might have the back four and two midfielders playing against the forwards.

Most weeks would follow a similar pattern and it wasn't uncommon for youth-team players to do two sessions a day and then our jobs after we'd finished, so I was often shattered when I got home. Monday sessions would usually be quite light, with Tuesday and Wednesday often being the most demanding days. Once you hit Wednesday you'd start to build into your match at the weekend unless you were playing midweek too, in which case everything would be more focused around recovery. On Thursdays we'd be at college all day and on a Friday morning we'd usually just play five-a-side, which was arguably the most enjoyable time of the week.

We'd sometimes play England vs the Rest of the World five-a-side, which could get interesting, or they'd carve The Cliff up into smaller pitches and mix everyone from the apprentices, reserves and the first team up into teams. It was brilliant because you could find yourself playing in the same side as your heroes and mixing it with solid pros who had been around the block.

They were fantastic experiences that helped you get adjusted to the pace things happen at a higher level and you had to learn quickly. I remember getting a shoulder charge from Mark Hughes that left me flat on my face, it was like running into a bus! Norman Whiteside was quality and always seemed to have time on the ball. Honestly, we could have played on a postage stamp and he'd have found some space on it, he was that good. He had a fantastic football brain and was incredibly sharp. Norman was a top guy too; on a Monday afternoon all the apprentices would be getting on with our jobs after training. When I was doing the kit I used to jump on the minibus over to Old Trafford from The Cliff, which took about 15 minutes, but one day he spotted me as he was coming out of the dressing room and offered me a lift. I nervously climbed into the passenger seat of his pale blue Jag. He was an established first-team player but didn't look down on me, asking how I was getting on at college and about my tutor, who he remembered from his own time there. He told me to keep going with my studies because it was important, and with how things turned out for both of us in our careers he wasn't wrong. It was quite special really and I felt ten foot tall when we reached Old Trafford.

All the first-team players were extremely grounded and I used to observe them to see how they went about their business. You'd see the likes of Mike Phelan and Micky Duxbury helping the kitman with the skip off the coach, which you'd never see modern players doing in a million years, and it said a lot about them as people and where they'd come from. Old-school values.

After a while you occasionally found yourself called over to train with them, which was another special experience. You just tried to do your best and not show yourself up. You had to be on it or you'd struggle to get a touch and would be running all over the place. They'd kick you and sometimes you could sense that they didn't really want to give you the ball in case you had a bad touch or lost it.

Some players make that step up purely on talent. I remember Ryan Giggs skinning Viv Anderson a few times in a practice match but it's harder when you haven't got as much ability to gain their respect because there were some big characters in there. There are levels in football like there are in other sports or walks of life and I was still quite green at the time. It used to be daunting going into their dressing room as they were your heroes but you had to get over that quickly because by putting them on a pedestal you were putting yourself at a disadvantage.

Things could boil over from time to time too, so you had to be careful. There was a lad in our year called Stevie Carter, a tricky right-winger from Hartlepool and a nice lad. He said something to Steve Bruce once, who wasn't going to take that from an apprentice and had him by the scruff of the neck!

They wouldn't take any shit but on the whole they were absolutely brilliant, with most of them coming from working-class backgrounds or through the youth system themselves, so they could relate to us and I can't remember many big egos. Paul Ince was maybe one exception. Personally I got on with him and he used to call me 'Tonga' but he was an extrovert who had a lot of front and self-belief. I remember him telling the canteen girls at The Cliff that his watch was worth more than their house, which was his way of bantering them. I think he also had a car registration plate with 'GUV 1' on it. I'm not sure the manager would have been overly enthused with that.

The way The Cliff was set up you'd have the first team, reserves and apprentices all in the same building, so it was tight-knit like a big family. It was a special place with an aura around it and you could almost feel the ghosts of those that had gone before in the corridors or the changing rooms just like at Old Trafford. The Busby Babes and George Best honed their craft there so you were following in their footsteps.

I can still picture the layout of it all now more than 30 years later. Outside was the main pitch where the first team would usually train and the rest of us would get the minibus over to Littleton Road. We'd often play our home matches for the 'A' team there though, and it still has an old stand on the far side, which we mainly just used for shelter in bad weather.

At the top was a small pitch we called 'Little Wembley' because it was always in pristine condition. We'd go up there to practise crossing and finishing or play five-a-side, which provided some great memories. There was also the indoor Astro, which had a pitch about two-thirds the size of a full one and where it always seemed to be colder than it was outside.

Inside downstairs were three dressing rooms split into first team, reserves and youth team; the boot room with its pigeonholes and smell of dubbin; and a kit room, which had washing machines and tumble dryers with muddy and washed kit piled high. There was a noticeboard at the bottom of the stairs where on a Friday afternoon the teams would be pinned up for that weekend's fixtures. Eric Harrison would shout, 'Teams up!' and we'd all excitedly rush to get a look at where we'd be playing. It was a buzz if you saw you'd been moved up a team or picked to go with the reserves, which could include the opportunity of playing on the hallowed turf at Old Trafford.

Upstairs was the gaffer's office, coaches' room, and the canteen where we'd all eat dinner together after training. It had two drinks machines, one for milk and the other for orange juice, so they were always very convenient after a tough training session. There was a coaches' table but other than that everyone sat together so you'd quite often find yourself having dinner next to one of your heroes, which was as terrifying as it was exciting. When it came to the food served there was no inkling for nutrition. We'd be eating bangers and mash, fish and chips on a Friday lunch with chocolate pudding to finish off, usually with custard. It was the norm back then and I don't think it really started to change until Eric Cantona arrived a few years later. No wonder some of us were blowing like a train in the Saturday morning youth-team matches!

The physio room was also upstairs and wasn't somewhere I spent a great deal of time because I never had any serious injuries, maybe just the usual ankle sprains and swelling that would have kept me out for a few weeks. Like at every club, though, it was the heartbeat of the training ground. In the morning the coaches would stick their head in to get an idea of who was injured and unable to train that day.

The physio Jim McGregor was a real character with a thick Scottish accent and he had a bit of a stutter too. He had a great personality, very bubbly and full of humour. I think in that role you need to be really because often lads who are injured will be very downbeat, so the banter is much needed. It's not an easy job – there's a lot of science behind it and knowledge required – but he was held in high regard by everyone at the club.

There was a gym, which only had high windows to let the light in. There were some weights in there, wall bars, a couple of exercise bikes and an old-fashioned weighing scale. It sometimes had a table tennis table set up and a ball attached to the end of a rope that you could practise your heading with.

Overall the facilities and methods employed were pretty basic but elements of science were tentatively starting to creep into the game even if they were often viewed with some suspicion. I remember a nutritionist coming in and speaking to all the players about the importance of a healthy diet. They were promoting the benefits of chopped-up apples, bananas, nuts, grapes, raisins and sultanas when Billy Garton piped up, 'How do you eat all that, stick it in a nosebag?' Cue laughter.

Gordon Strachan was very fit and played until he was 40. He once brought a load of seaweed tablets in and tried to get everyone on them. The only problem was that when you went to the toilet they turned your piss a luminous green colour.

Archie Knox used to be obsessed with pressure points all over the body and have us rubbing our legs after we'd finished training to help aid recovery. I think it was related to acupuncture or something like that and someone somewhere must have seen some value in it.

Sports science was in its infancy though, and the drinking culture was still rife in football, not just at United but pretty much every club. It was part and parcel of the game and you'd occasionally see a couple of the first-team players coming into training slightly worse for wear. I remember Ralph Milne used to get two battered fish after a night out but eat them the next morning, probably to sober himself up. He also had this odd habit of tucking his ears into themselves when he was training, maybe so he couldn't hear the gaffer and Archie Knox. If you saw him at a glance you'd think he didn't have any! I'm not sure whether he used Blu Tack or even why he did it – I never asked.

As a young player you're only as good as the senior players in your dressing room, and if they're out getting hammered a lot that's what you're going to pick up too. There was a curfew of sorts, an unwritten rule that you couldn't go out within 48 hours of a match, but whether any of them broke it is another matter.

It does make a difference because it dehydrates you, and even a couple of pints can take the edge off you in training. It was something that the gaffer was eager to stamp out, but a problem for him was Whiteside, McGrath and Bryan Robson, his captain, were three major players for United at the time and allegedly some of the biggest drinkers.

Robbo was a great trainer and one of the fittest at the club. He was one of those players who could have quite a bit to drink on a night out yet still be leading the pack the next morning. He must have been so naturally fit, coupled with always training hard, which meant he could get away with it. It's not like it hindered him in any way either because how could Bryan Robson have been any better? He was God in everyone's eyes, and rightly so.

It starts to catch up with some players eventually because their metabolism changes and they start putting weight on, but not Robbo, who played until he was 40. He was as fit as a butcher's dog and a brilliant bloke. He'd often come into the youth-team dressing room with a load of New Balance gear, which he'd leave on the table in the middle for us to help ourselves. He kept an eye out for everybody and would always chat to the younger players, taking an interest in us and our development.

My youth team-mate Kieran Toal told me a story a while ago about how he borrowed a pair of Robbo's boots for a pre-season match once, only to leave them on the bus going home. Poor Toaly spent the rest of the weekend sick with worry, dreading going in to training on the Monday morning because he'd lost the Manchester United and England captain's boots! He needn't have worried though, because when he broke the news to Robbo the response he got was typical of the man: 'Don't worry Toaly, these things happen.'

On one occasion I remember Robbo asking Eric Harrison whether he could borrow some of us to play in a tournament on a Sunday morning at Oldham Athletic's ground, Boundary Park. He was involved in the hotel business on the side and it was a seven-a-side competition between local hospitality firms formerly known as the Willoughby Hotels Challenge Cup. Robbo had a bet with one of his mates that the team entered for his hotel chain would win the trophy, which we did at a canter, but what no one knew was we were actually the Manchester United youth team! We absolutely played everyone off the park because we were up against lads who were chefs, receptionists or kitchen porters in their day jobs.

My dad came down to watch and sat near Robbo in the stands, who was absolutely creasing himself, watching it all unfold. There was me, Micky Pollitt, Mark Gordon, Marcus Brameld, Paul Sixsmith, Kieran Toal and Jimmy Shields involved, and we all got a little picture with Robbo and the trophy at the end, which I've still got.

We were also lucky enough to get the opportunity to play alongside him on a couple of occasions when he came and played in 'A' team fixtures against Crewe and Rochdale reserves while coming back from injury. It was unbelievable to see how he prepared and, like a lot of top players, his temperament was bang-on. Nothing really fazed him; he was very cold and almost assassin-like. He used to rub Vaseline on to his eyebrows pre-match and it dawned on me that he was preparing to put his head in where it hurt. He was going to war basically, and would run until he dropped – what a man.

I remember us kicking off in the Crewe match, and for the first few minutes you'd just expect him to play his way in and get on the ball a little bit, but he absolutely smashed one of their players over the line in the first five minutes and you could see he wasn't going to take it easy. He played how he would for the first team and it was an amazing experience to share a pitch with my hero.

Chapter 5

Fledgling

I MUST have been doing something right because on 19 January 1989, just over six months into my apprenticeship and still only 16 years old, I made my debut for Manchester United reserves as a substitute for Jules Maiorana in a 7-1 victory over West Brom at Old Trafford. I was still very young, especially for a defender, but there was plenty of experience on hand. Gordon Strachan played and was coming towards the end of his time at the club, as was Paul McGrath, who captained us that night, so I was in esteemed company.

Mark Robins scored a hat-trick and Shaun Goater chipped in with a brace to give us a comfortable win. It's a little-known fact that Shaun was at United as a youngster and many fans I speak to are surprised by that. I think he likes to distance himself from it to avoid detracting from his legendary status with the blue side of Manchester. I remember him as a really good player who scored quite a lot of goals in the reserves and junior teams. Like a lot of us though, you got the impression that the culture at the club didn't really allow him to express himself fully. He was very laid-back and I think the coaches thought he wasn't as serious as he should have been. It didn't work out for him but he ended up going to Rotherham and doing really well there before getting his big move to City.

Reserve-team football was a step up from the 'A' or 'B' teams and it was exciting. Tony Morley, who had won the European Cup with Aston Villa, played on the left wing for West Brom so that was a good test for me that I was able to build on in a handful more appearances before the end of the season, which included starts against Blackburn Rovers and Barnsley.

I used to love it when I was in the youth-team dressing room at The Cliff before training and the reserves manager Brian Whitehouse would stick his head round the door and say, 'You're coming with me this morning, Tongey.' It gave me a little boost because it felt like you were getting the recognition and progressing to the next level. I liked Brian a lot; he was a bit more laid-back than Eric Harrison and I think he saw something in me.

Our team at that level was a mixture of young lads coming through and experienced players who either weren't in the first team or were coming back from injury. It was a great education for a young player and the Central League was a better bridge to the first team than the current age-group-based system with under-21s, because the standard was decent and it gave you the opportunity to play against some top players.

I remember playing against Norman Whiteside after he'd moved to Everton, and I came directly up against Peter Beagrie in the same match. He was a tricky player and a nightmare to mark because when you went to block the cross on one side he'd just chop back on his other foot. There was Neil Lennon, Andy Hinchcliffe, Michael Hughes and David White turning out for Manchester City, and our matches against them were fiercely contested, like they were in the junior teams, but great experiences.

I also remember coming up against the late Gary Speed when we played Leeds on Old Trafford, Martin Keown for Everton and Ian Rush within Liverpool's reserve team.

Quite a few of the older lads who were already established in the reserves did make the step up to first-team level with mixed success. Deiniol Graham and David Wilson both played a handful of times for Manchester United. Derek Brazil got a couple of games as did Paul Wratten, while Mark Robins and Russell Beardsmore both played about 70 matches each.

I played a few times with Tony Gill, who was a quality full-back or midfielder and had started to make an impact in about a dozen first-team appearances before a bad tackle ended his career. He tried to come back but had a tough rehab, with loads of scars on his leg, and he just couldn't quite get there, which was really sad. Those lads were what became known as the first batch of 'Fergie's Fledglings', the forerunners of the Class of '92, so there were young players getting some opportunities and the ressies was a good springboard for that.

It was also another opportunity to play alongside some of your heroes and see how they prepared for matches, including the likes of Whiteside, McGrath, Strachan and Steve Bruce in competitive fixtures on big grounds such as Goodison Park, Bramall Lane, Villa Park and Old Trafford, a few times under the lights, which was always nice.

I remember cutting my eye open in one match against Newcastle and Steve Bruce telling the physio to hang fire until we'd defended a corner. I had blood trickling down my face and all over my shirt. My head was spinning but he was barking, 'Tongey, get on that back post, the physio can wait a minute!' Brucey bled for the cause on more than one occasion so obviously us defending a set piece was more important than me getting the necessary treatment. Like I say, different times and a different culture.

It threw up some good away trips too, even if the football itself sometimes left something to be desired. I remember a couple of friendlies against Barnet when Barry Fry was the manager there, in one of which they beat us 4-1 on their old ground at Underhill. I was in the squad but didn't get on, thankfully, which probably saved me from the hairdryer treatment, unlike the rest of the lads who would have got both barrels.

There was a match at non-league Flixton where United sent a representative team, which included Clayton Blackmore and Lee Martin, for the grand opening of their new floodlights. They were definitely needed on a dark, dull evening on which we won by a single goal on a mess of a pitch. It was a typical non-league ground with tiny changing rooms that were cold and muddy. It passed me by at the time but I've still got the programme from that match and it was sponsored by 'David Herd Motors', a car sales business owned by the former United striker who was prolific for a few seasons in the 60s. Growing up, my dad used to rave about 'Hotshot Herd', which was the name given to him by supporters due to the number of goals he scored with his fierce shot.

I remember a series of pre-season friendlies where I came on for Billy Garton in three or four consecutive matches. He must have been sick of shaking my hand! We also played Liverpool and Everton's reserves in a triangular tournament in Cornwall one year, called the Studio Ten Challenge Trophy. United are pretty well supported down there so our matches attracted reasonable crowds and we took a decent squad that included the likes of Mark Bosnich, Colin Gibson, Ralph Milne, Jules Maiorana and Deiniol Graham. If my memory serves me right we stayed at a hotel called

The Green Lawns and I roomed with a lad called Raphael Burke, who was a talented winger.

The tournament itself didn't go that well. I was an unused substitute against Everton, which ended in a draw. I started against Liverpool, who beat us, and I sadly picked up a groin strain early on. At the reception after the match I remember hearing Darren Ferguson arguing with some of their lads, telling them his dad was a millionaire, and me rolling my eyes. We also watched a stand-up routine from the Cornish comedian Jethro, which was very funny.

Probably the most memorable trip was a visit to the Isle of Man. We got the plane over there, which was obviously only a short flight but an awful one in poor weather conditions where we were packed in like sardines on a tiny aircraft that went at such a slow speed it felt like you could put your hand in the propeller. The match was held at the Douglas Bowl, which wasn't a bad little ground, with a decent crowd. It was a very windy day and I think Mark Bosnich got caught out by it from a cross, but the goal must have been disallowed because we won convincingly 6-0.

Norman Whiteside was in the squad and got on the scoresheet. He was coming to the end of his time at United as injuries took their toll but was still a brilliant player and a top guy too, who bought us all a drink afterwards. I've still got the newspaper report from the match and it was an honour to be representing Manchester United alongside him, even if it wasn't quite at first-team level.

I was only 17, finding my way, and he was a few years older but had already achieved some great things in the game. I remember watching the FA Cup Final in 1985 where he curled the winning goal past Neville Southall, so to be playing alongside him in a United shirt just four years later was very surreal and a dream come true in many ways.

I think some of the more experienced players like Norman probably saw the reserves as a bit of a graveyard, especially if they'd fallen out of favour with the gaffer, but it gave me some great experiences over a couple of runs in the team. It was difficult to establish yourself because if Viv Anderson, for example, didn't play in the first team and wasn't injured, he'd probably play in the reserves at right-back, which was my position. As a young lad how can you compete with an England international and European Cup winner? There was competition for places throughout the club, and if the experienced pros weren't in the first team they needed to be housed somewhere, which meant I was often relegated back down to the 'A' team.

The ressies provided me with one of my favourite memories at United when I helped set up a goal for Mark Robins to seal a 2-1 win over Liverpool on Old Trafford under the lights. I came on for Lee Martin and remember getting down the side and putting in some good work for Mark to volley home. It was a great moment, to do it against Liverpool, especially in front of the Stretford End, and I've still got the newspaper cutting with the write-up by David Meek in the *Manchester Evening News*, which was just brilliant. Great memories.

Chapter 6

Behind the Iron Curtain

'SO YOU'RE gonna need ten tins of beans, a pack of toilet rolls and a box of cornflakes.'

I got the opportunity to broaden my horizons in the spring of 1989 when I was selected for two different representative teams to play on both home and foreign soil. The first was as part of an FA XI against an England schools team played at York Street, the home of Boston United. My mates Micky Pollitt and Jason Lydiate were involved from United and there were some lads in the squad who went on to have decent careers – Lee Clark, Steve Harkness, Des Lyttle, Simon Charlton and Steve McManaman.

I played directly against McManaman a few times for United's 'A' team. He was a tricky player and I've still got a referee's report somewhere from one match at The Cliff where I was booked for a tackle on him, which reads, 'In the 10th minute, Tonge the United number two raised his boot in a dangerous manner and caught McManaman the Liverpool number eleven just below the windpipe.' It was nothing personal, other than the fact that he played for the enemy, and I remember chatting to him on the train down to the match. I can't remember much about the match itself other than getting a bollocking from Eric Harrison when I got back to United, as his scout had told him I didn't get over the halfway line. Typical.

The second trip a few weeks later was more memorable and came as a bit of a surprise because it involved a trip to Moscow as part of a Football League XI to celebrate the centenary, with a match against our Russian counterparts. United must have put my name forward and Archie Knox called me into the office. He said they were sending me to Russia and to make sure I packed plenty of cornflakes, tinned food and toilet rolls!

I had to get the train down to London on my own, which was pretty daunting, as was finding my way to the hotel where we were staying in the big smoke before flying out from Heathrow. Alan Ball and Lawrie McMenemy were the joint managers of the team and I remember meeting Bally for the first time after I'd just about made it to the hotel. He was in the foyer reading a copy of *Sporting Life* as I sat down nervously and a little bit starstruck. I was a shy 17-year-old lad and here I was meeting a World Cup winner, about to play in a team being managed by him. Lawrie was also a decent guy with a good personality, very down to earth and they say he was close to getting the England manager's job at one point.

It was a good group of lads on the trip and I ended up being made captain despite being the youngest member of the squad; the rest of the lads were a year or two older. Steve Round was there; he, of course, was David Moyes's assistant during his ill-fated spell in charge of United, but at the time he was a very quiet lad on the books at Derby County. There was a lad from Oldham Athletic called Simon Mooney, Carl Griffiths played for Manchester City, Paul Tait was a talented player at Birmingham City and Darren Garner from Plymouth Argyle, who I'd later cross swords with in a Devon derby. There was also Dane Whitehouse from Sheffield

United, Paul Kitson, who played in the Premier League, and Joey Beauchamp played a few hundred times for Oxford United, but he sadly passed away in 2022.

A trip to Russia in the 1980s was quite an intimidating prospect. I'd grown up in the height of the Cold War and the country wasn't in the best of states at the time with the fall of communism approaching. I remember seeing stony-faced people queueing up for bread, and the architecture was grey. The place was cold in more ways than one and generally a bit grim. The hotel wasn't the best either, with thin, scratchy woollen blankets on the beds, and the food was shocking. We were served soup for breakfast one day that had an egg in the middle of it. In fairness to Archie Knox, he wasn't that far wide of the mark.

There were a few FA dignitaries with us, and George Scanlan, an interpreter who later assisted Eric Cantona and Andrei Kanchelskis when they came to United. They took us to visit the sights in Moscow, including Red Square with all the coloured domes, and the Kremlin. I remember going to Lenin's tomb and Bally pointing out all the weeds around it in his squeaky voice. You'd have thought it would have been immaculate.

The match was played at the Luzhniki Stadium, which of course was the scene of United's Champions League Final triumph over Chelsea nearly two decades later. It had definitely been modernised by then though, because we trained on the pitch there the day before and I remember thinking the place was in keeping with the rest of Russia – depressing. The pitch was bobbly and the groundsman was cutting the grass with an old scythe. Imagine *Escape to Victory* meets *Rocky IV*.

We wore black armbands for the Hillsborough disaster that had tragically occurred only a few days before. I'd been playing for United's 'A' team over at Accrington on the day of the tragedy, where we beat Stanley's reserves 1-0. We were first told about it as we came off the pitch.

We beat our Russian counterparts, who were a representative team largely made up of players from Moscow's biggest clubs, 2-1 in front of a reasonable crowd. They were quite direct but I remember feeling that we were the better team. The technical standard of their players wasn't that great and we were getting quite a few chances.

I've still got the shirt I wore for the match and, looking back, it was an interesting experience to go away from home comforts to captain a team in a foreign country that culturally was totally different to the UK. As skipper I had to give a speech to the rest of the group on the plane journey home and I think I spoke for everybody when I said, 'I've really enjoyed the trip and I'd love to go on another, but to a different place.'

Chapter 7

46 minutes at Histon

EVER SINCE I was a kid standing on the terrace at Old Trafford with my dad or watching them in cup finals on TV my dream had been to play for Manchester United. Most young lads who grow up obsessed with football dream of playing for their boyhood club but very few get the chance to do it. So imagine my excitement when at the end of my first year as an apprentice in May 1989 I was included in the first-team squad for an end-of-season friendly at Histon.

The match had been arranged as part of the deal to bring Giuliano Maiorana to United about six months earlier. 'Jules' was an exceptionally talented winger who had been plucked from non-league obscurity, and the transfer had saved Histon from going out of business. It must have been a strange transition for him coming from part-time football, and just a few weeks later he was playing in Manchester United's first team, but he took it all in his stride.

It was *Roy of the Rovers* stuff really; he'd played in a televised 1-1 draw against Arsenal at Old Trafford that season and given Lee Dixon the runaround, so there was a lot of hype around him. He was a good-looking Italian lad with several tricks at his disposal, and regularly had me on toast in practice matches. He was quite tall for a winger and would flick the ball over you with his heel.

Jules was another one who didn't quite fit in with the culture at the club because he hadn't come through the youth system and had been brought up to have his own mind. He was a good lad who was very grounded but hadn't been institutionalised like the rest of us. I think he saw the harshness, bullying and belittling of people and was a strong enough personality not to go along with it.

He'd stand his ground, which didn't go down well at all with the coaching staff, and there was definitely a personality clash between him and the gaffer. Coaches like players that they can control but Jules was his own person who stood by his morals and ethics when it probably would have been easier to go with the flow. I respected him for that.

He played a few times for the first team before a bad knee injury, and his difficult relationship with the manager prevented him progressing. By the time he eventually left the club at the end of 1993/94 he was a forgotten man.

I'd only turned 17 a few months before and was quite nervous reporting to Old Trafford. I clambered on to the coach and sat down, trying to keep myself to myself. Steve Bruce got on shortly after and as he was walking down the aisle said to me, 'Tongey, you can't sit there. That's the gaffer's table where he plays cards.' Not a great start, so I started to get my bag to move, when the gaffer boarded the coach while I was desperately trying to get off his table. Quick as a flash I just heard Brucey quip, 'Gaffer, Tongey's sat in your seat and he says he's not fucking moving!'

Honestly, my heart rate went through the roof. 'Aye, you will fucking move, son.'

We travelled down to the match, which was to be played at Cambridge United's Abbey Stadium, with most of the lads listening to their Walkman or playing those old electronic games, which were very basic and of their time. We stopped off at a hotel near the ground in the afternoon for the pre-match meal, which was either beans or egg on toast.

It was a thrill to be part of the group because it was a strong squad that travelled. Our coach had a police escort to the ground with a motorbike leading the way, so I remember sitting there thinking this was bigger than anything I'd experienced before. In the dressing room beforehand the senior players such as Steve Bruce and Micky Duxbury were giving out plenty of advice to the younger lads and telling us to enjoy it; just being good pros really, and it was appreciated.

The starting XI that night read: Leighton, Martin, Sharpe, Bruce, Duxbury, Donaghy, Blackmore, Beardsmore, Toal, Hughes and Maiorana. It was a decent team with quite a few young lads, including myself, Sean McAuley, Paul Sixsmith, Jason Lydiate, Darren Ferguson, Wayne Bullimore and Simon Andrews on the bench.

My chance came when Lee Martin picked up an injury just before half-time and limped off, so I entered the fray. I remember Mark Hughes sold me short with a pass early on after he'd held the ball up like he always did, and I had to slide in to keep possession.

The pitch was a bit bumpy, with not much grass on it – a typical end-of-season playing surface in those days, but I did alright, showing some nice touches and making a few tackles. You were playing with the big boys now and it was a level up from the standard I was used to in the 'A' team. Steve Bruce was at centre-half, and I remember him talking to me throughout, giving little nuggets of advice, and I certainly didn't let myself down.

We won 3-1 with goals from my youth team-mate Kieran Toal, Clayton Blackmore and Mark Hughes. It was an enjoyable experience that I'll never forget, in front of a decent crowd of just under 4,000 and a great atmosphere. There was a little pitch invasion at the end with the locals clamouring to get the United players' autographs. I was sent a video of the match a couple of years ago, which is a reminder that I had a bit more hair back then, and it was surreal watching it back. I've also still got the annual yearbook from that season where the match is listed under 'first team – other'.

I seem to remember that the gaffer didn't hang around afterwards and was keen to get back to Manchester. The reserves were having a difficult season that year and needed to win their last match to avoid being relegated from the Central League. I was at Old Trafford to watch them beat Coventry City 4-0 the next day with a strong team and I think, looking back, his mind was probably on that. The following Monday I was back to sweeping dressing rooms and cleaning boots with the other apprentices to keep our feet well and truly on the ground, earning every penny of my £29.50 a week.

Maybe the timing wasn't the best, with it being the end of the season. If it had been a few months earlier and the first team had experienced an injury crisis shortly after I might have got another opportunity. In those days you were only allowed a couple of subs so it was very difficult to get a look-in. I've still got a picture of all the contracted players in a squad photo at Old Trafford from that 1988/89 season, and there's loads of us! There are about 50 or 60 players on there so that was the level of competition you were up against. You had to be outstanding to even be knocking on the door and then exceptional to earn the manager's trust.

It's a great memory to look back on though. I think there's only something like 1,500 players who have played for Manchester United's first team in competitive matches or friendlies and to have played a very small part in that is something I'll always be proud of. Paul Scholes once said that if he got to play only one match with United's first team that would have been more than enough. It's a phrase I'd have to live out!

The beauty of life is that when you're living it you don't really get the chance to appreciate it for what it is. It's natural when you've had a taste of something to want more or even expect it, but things often don't work out the way you want them to. At 17 you're young, invincible and think your time will come, but what you don't realise is this could be as good as it gets.

Chapter 8

Giggsy and the Doc

'SEE THAT kid over there? He's going to be some player, that lad.' I still remember the first time I saw Ryan Giggs play.

I was getting ready to take part in another schoolboy training session one evening at The Cliff when Eric Harrison came over and pointed out a spindly lad playing with another group on the AstroTurf. Ryan would have only been about 13. He was very thin and, going off his physical appearance, didn't really look like much. I wouldn't have taken too much notice anyway as I was only around 14 or 15 myself.

He was Ryan Wilson then, of course, before he changed his name. We only found that out when he came with the youth team to play in the Grossi-Morera tournament in Italy a couple of years later while still at school. They had this protocol where before a match the officials would come into the dressing room, read out each player's name and check their passport.

'Ryan Giggs.'

I remember sitting there looking around with everyone else, wondering whether there was a new lad in the squad that we'd not been told about, but then Ryan stood up and that was the first we knew of it. Of course, when it was my turn they pronounced my name as 'Alan Tonje', which led to me being mercilessly ripped by Brian Kidd for ages afterwards. He'd do this routine where he'd shout my name as they pronounced it and stand to attention, thinking it was hilarious.

Giggsy was great to play alongside and had a good left foot, coupled with a great burst of pace that allowed him to drop his shoulder and get past defenders, causing them all kinds of problems. He had quick feet and was like a gazelle because he didn't carry any weight on him at all. He was also very intelligent with the runs he made. He'd often come towards the ball then spin, so if you could deliver it over the top of the defender he could get in behind like a whippet. It meant that he could do a very good job playing as a centre-forward if required because his bending runs and movement patterns were so effective.

What set Ryan apart, though, was his mentality, because nothing seemed to faze him. He was very down to earth and didn't say a lot but you could see he was confident in himself; his persona was almost cold and assassin-like.

On a Friday afternoon the team sheets for all the matches the next day would be pinned up at The Cliff on the noticeboard at the bottom of the stairs. When I got home, my dad would always ask me who I was playing for and which other lads were playing in my team. If I told him I'd be playing with Giggsy his eyes would always light up. I think he was more excited about watching Ryan than me!

United probably had him destined for stardom at an early age and the path was laid out in front of him. The George Best comparisons started early, which, although inevitable because there was definitely a resemblance, were maybe a bit unfair, so the gaffer was quick to discourage them. It wasn't all plain sailing for him, though, as he got a lot of grief from Eric Harrison, and I believe that continued from the gaffer when he got into the first team. I remember walking back across the car park at The Cliff with him one day and he was close to tears. I think Eric had been on his back after a bad performance or something, and I just said to him, 'Keep going Ryan, don't worry about it. You're a good player and you'll be alright.' I'm not sure whether Ryan will remember that but I can recall it clearly and I wasn't wrong, to be fair.

He made his first-team debut at 17 in March 1991 against Everton at Old Trafford but I wasn't there to witness it because I was playing in the reverse fixture for the reserves at Goodison Park. He only played a couple of times that season as they gradually eased him in, but he broke through properly in 1991/92. The rest as they say is history and he was dynamite over the next few years – the goal against Spurs, the one at QPR away and dribbling past all the Arsenal players at Villa Park before revealing the Axminster rug on his chest during the treble season! He had some career considering the number of trophies won and the longevity. He's got to be in the mix when you're talking about United's greatest-ever player. The older generation will say George Best all day but Ryan wasn't bad, was he?

Our paths have crossed a couple of times since he eventually retired in 2014. I interviewed him for a podcast I'd set up called 'I can't explain' and asked what kept him going for so long. He just said it was about standards, which influenced how he behaved every day in training and fed into the mentality to do it day in, day out. There were a few listeners' questions sent in too.

'What was Alan Tonge like as a player?'

Moment of truth. 'Yeah, you were decent, a good player. You weren't lightning quick but you weren't slow either. When I played against you I always had to try and trick you because you knew your position well and never switched off.' Nice answer Ryan!

I went to a tribute dinner the former players' association at United held for him a few years ago at Old Trafford and got a copy of his book signed to put in a raffle for a relative whose daughter had tragically died from an asthma attack. That wasn't an easy task, as with him being the star exhibit I knew he'd have people around him all evening and it would be hard to talk to him. I don't know how but I managed to blag entry to the VIP area. I waited outside the lifts knowing he'd have to come up that way, while warding off the attention of the security guard by convincing him I was there legitimately. When the lift opened and Ryan appeared we had a little chat while he signed the book for me. He asked me what I was currently doing and then came out with, 'I must still owe you some petrol money.'

Humorously, I responded, 'With interest that must equate to a good few grand, Ryan.'

I used to pick him up at the bus stop opposite the bar 'Albert's' on the East Lancs Road on the way to training in my little beige Fiesta. It was nice he remembered that.

At another Man United ex-players' association event I was introduced to a diehard fan by Peter Bolton, who's a massive red himself, 'This is Alan Tonge. He used to play with Ryan Giggs before their careers went in very different directions.' Charming! Made me chuckle though, as it was meant with no malice. Lovely memories, and it's strange how things often work out. Destiny.

Everyone is familiar with the career of Ryan Giggs and what he achieved in the game. Fewer will be aware of the story of Adrian Doherty, who played on the opposite wing to Ryan in our youth team and was considered just as good at the time.

Aidy, or 'Doc', was a lovely lad who was completely unique and it would be fair to say he wasn't your typical footballer. He read books and poetry and listened to music that wouldn't have been the popular choice for a bunch of teenagers with their Walkmans. He was a Bob Dylan fanatic and would often give away his tickets to watch the first team at Old Trafford so he could go busking in Manchester city centre. He was a shy lad with a thick Northern Irish accent but he'd surprise you on occasion. At one of the Christmas pantomimes the youth team used to have to do an act for the first team and coaching staff. Doc played a guitar solo, 'The Times They Are A-Changin' by Bob Dylan. He was just stood up there: 'Come gather round people wherever you roam …' It was brilliant and brought the house down.

Everyone at the club loved him, including the first team. He was an interesting character and you wouldn't know what to expect from one day to the next. He'd turn up with his boots in a carrier bag or one of his shoes wouldn't have any laces in. On away trips he'd often just take himself off up to his room, but when he did appear at mealtimes he'd be wearing an old grandad-style vest and his slippers, while the rest of us were in our club tracksuits. I think there was an acceptance from the coaches that he was a bit different and they allowed it, probably to make him feel comfortable.

If you didn't know him and someone told you he was an up-and-coming prospect at United you wouldn't have believed them. He was small, and when he put his kit on it would be all baggy. There was nothing of him and he had a very pasty complexion, with freckles. If he was out in the sun for 20 minutes he'd come back in all red. He didn't look like a footballer at all but when you put a ball at his feet he was a different animal.

Doc was a star-quality player. Very quick and direct with two good feet. He was more of an old-fashioned winger in the mould of Stanley Matthews, liking the ball played into his feet so he could run at defenders. His pace was electric and, like Giggsy, he was so brave. Back then pitches weren't the greatest and wingers could come up against some very experienced full-backs who would try to batter them, but he never stopped asking for the ball. He had a lot of heart.

His pace and trickery were so difficult to deal with and it didn't matter who you were because he was fearless. I remember playing against Liverpool's 'A' team at Melwood and Steve Staunton was their left-back, but Aidy was unbelievable that morning against an established first-team player and international.

There was another match on a damp, grey morning at The Cliff where Alan Hansen was playing for Liverpool, probably on his way back from injury. I was injured myself but went to watch and witnessed our lads thrash them 5-1 and Hansen bulleting a header past his own goalkeeper from a corner. My dad was there and swears to this day he did it on purpose out of frustration. Aidy was on fire that day, causing havoc, and it was a good scalp for the lads.

As someone else who didn't really fit with the dressing room culture, we had a good relationship. I'm not saying I shared his interests or we were particularly close but we got on and it helped that I played right-back behind him a lot, so we formed a nice little partnership on the pitch too. I liked to get stuck in, whereas he was more creative, so a lot of the time I'd win the ball and give it to him to do his thing.

We had Giggsy on the left and Doc on the right and the noise was beginning to grow around the club. There's a certain romanticism with wingers at United because the fans love that rawness of youth and a player who gets you off your seat. It's continued right through to the modern day with the buzz around Alejandro Garnacho in recent times.

There was a sense that Ryan Giggs and Adrian Doherty would be the next two to break into the Manchester United first team and it was only a matter of time before one or both of them was given a chance. I've still got some newspaper cuttings and I think David Meek from the *Manchester Evening News* picked up on it. I remember Aidy getting likened to Johnny Berry, and he'd already travelled with the first team to a match at Southampton away as cover.

The dogs were barking, but just as he appeared to be on the verge of getting an opportunity, a cruel twist of fate intervened. He suffered a knee injury in an 'A' team match against Carlisle United reserves, the dreaded cruciate, just a week or two before he was supposedly going to make his debut in what turned out to be the match against Everton where Giggsy made his. It stopped him progressing and maybe impacted his speed. The thing about football is that it moves on very quickly, and the likes of David Beckham and Keith Gillespie had overtaken him by the time he was able to get back on the pitch. After a couple of largely unsuccessful comeback attempts United released him in the summer of 1993 and his departure went unnoticed.

He had a brief spell with Derry City in the League of Ireland before drifting out of the game but he could have walked away from it anytime I think. That was the thing with Aidy, even if he hadn't been injured he might have played once in the first team, or a few more, then decided he was off to America to travel with a band or something. He was very off-the-cuff and I don't think he'd have had the same longevity that we saw with Giggsy. He was a drifter.

I think Aidy liked playing football but I'm not sure he loved it because he had other interests. It was probably difficult for the management to pin him down because he had his own free will and they probably had more control over Ryan. Their personalities were polar opposites and I think Ryan was very driven in his outlook, but football wasn't the be-all and end-all for Aidy, who had different components to his identity.

The story goes that the club offered them both five-year professional contracts but Doc would only sign for three because he wasn't sure football was what he wanted to be doing in a few years' time. That's crazy when you think about it and I can only imagine what the gaffer must have thought.

After leaving football behind he worked various jobs in a few different places but tragically died in an accident after slipping and falling into a canal shortly after moving to the Netherlands in 2000. He couldn't swim, unfortunately, and passed away the day before his 27th birthday. His life is portrayed in a book called *Forever Young*, written by the journalist Oliver Kay, which is a brilliant account and a great read.

I have very fond memories of him and I'm still in touch with his dad Jimmy, who's a lovely man. He still feels to this day that his son wasn't looked after by United with the medical procedures for the operation on his knee and the environment in digs, which he hated that much he ended up moving out and going to live with a family over in Levenshulme.

Their football careers and ultimately their lives ended up on very different paths but I think it's fair to say that Ryan Giggs and Adrian Doherty were both legends in their own right, and it was a pleasure to play alongside them both in a United shirt.

Chapter 9

The Class of 1990

IT'S A big thing to represent Manchester United in the FA Youth Cup. You feel the weight of history when you put on that shirt, and if you're not careful it can weigh you down. Every club wants to beat United and teams often raise their game, so there's a lot of pressure on you to deliver performances. If you can't handle it then you won't last long.

Every year when it came round you could sense a different vibe around the club. It was a big deal because of the club's record in the competition with the Busby Babes, and you were very aware of what you were representing.

My first experience of the competition came as a first-year apprentice in 1988/89. The club had been knocked out in the second round by Mansfield Town the previous year so the pressure was really on and a repeat performance unthinkable. Our opening tie was a tricky one up at Darlington on a cold December night. Their old ground at Feethams was next to a cricket pitch that was in much better condition than the pitch we played on, and there were a lot of nerves beforehand, with Eric Harrison all tensed up. I felt immense pride wearing the United shirt as I warmed up. An incredible feeling.

I was picked at centre-half and it was a good battle in front of a raucous crowd. We went 2-0 up before they came roaring back to level it at 2-2. We managed to get on top near the end with Wayne Bullimore scoring a free kick to secure a 5-2 victory, and I think relief was the overriding feeling afterwards, as we'd come through a strong test of our character in a real scrap.

It was a learning curve for us, which only steepened in the next round with a trip to play Sheffield Wednesday at Hillsborough. I remember walking out of the tunnel and being amazed by the ground. It was quite a daunting prospect to play on such a historic pitch. It was another battle and a very tight match that ended in a goalless draw. There weren't many chances at either end, and my stand-out memory is Sean McAuley fracturing his rib. The medical science at the time wasn't great because the physio came on the pitch and tried to get him to lift his arms up, thinking he was just winded. It was only when poor Sean was taken to hospital that they found out it was quite serious because it had also punctured his lung!

We beat them 2-0 in the replay at Old Trafford with goals from Simon Andrews and Wayne Bullimore. It really was a dream to play on that hallowed turf and it had such a great feel with all the floodlights on. There was a certain romance about it and you felt like a proper player. It was so exciting. My mum still says she can remember the buzz walking to the ground, with the mist and the floodlights on before the pride of seeing my name up in lights on the electronic scoreboard while they were reading out the line-ups.

The gaffer would often come to watch and occasionally a couple of the first-team players too. My dad remembers sitting near Wilf McGuinness at one match, and there was a bloke ranting and raving a few rows back. He could sense that Wilf was getting agitated. After a while he'd had enough and spun around in his seat: 'I get you on my television every night. It's called bloody interference!'

It was a great experience and we got to do it again in the next round when we put Ipswich Town away 4-1 in a comfortable win. I think Eric was pretty happy afterwards because their youth system had a decent reputation. Lee Sharpe made his first start in the competition, actually partnering me at centre-half. Sharpey had quite a buoyant personality and was very happy-go-lucky. He'd arrived from Torquay United and I remember him training with us a lot at first. He got in the first team quite young and, because he'd been signed externally, I think they kind of already had a pathway for him. It was still a time when young players who were already in and around the first-team squad would drop back down to play in the Youth Cup, which doesn't happen as often now.

Our next match, away at Brentford in the fifth round, was probably the most disappointing experience I had in football. It was another battle, at Griffin Park, and we thought we'd done enough to win it when Craig Lawton scored with just a few minutes remaining. He volleyed the ball into the roof of the net and I remember turning back towards our goal with my fists clenched, thinking we'd pinched it. The last five minutes turned into a nightmare. Brentford equalised and not long after went 2-1 up. I remember Roger Sallis getting a right bollocking from Eric Harrison afterwards as he'd tried to play offside. Khotso Moabi just nudged the ball past Mark Bosnich and I remember hurtling back as the ball was trickling towards the net in slow motion to try to save the day but not quite getting there. Moabi unfortunately broke his collarbone when all his team-mates jumped on him to celebrate their 2-1 victory, so maybe it wasn't the best night for him either.

We'd managed to snatch defeat from the jaws of victory and we were gutted. It was a real body blow to be knocked out like that. Fergie and Archie Knox had travelled down to London for the match and the hairdryer was on full blast afterwards. I remember them saying that only Simon Andrews and I had come out with any credit. Archie told Lee Sharpe that he wouldn't play for the first team ever again. It was madness!

We had a more positive experience about six months later when we travelled to play in the prestigious Grossi-Morera youth tournament in Italy. It was probably the equivalent of the modern-day UEFA Youth Champions League, and all the top young players in Europe were involved. I seem to remember Paulo Di Canio being in Lazio's squad and Alessandro Costacurta was playing for AC Milan, whereas we had the likes of Ryan Giggs and Adrian Doherty starting to come through, both of whom were on that trip.

There was a lock of Diego Maradona's hair in a frame at the hotel where we stayed. He was still playing for Napoli at the time and was revered as a god in Naples. Brian Kidd came with us and I remember him asking to borrow the tape of 'She Drives Me Crazy' by Fine Young Cannibals for his Walkman.

We were drawn in the same group as AC Milan, Napoli and Viterbo Select XI, which was tough on paper, but we were outstanding and beat all of them. The pitches weren't the best and we played one match on a shale surface, which wasn't great. In another there was a massive storm that flooded the pitch and the ball wasn't going anywhere, so we had to sit in the dressing room until it passed before play could resume.

Wins over Atalanta and Torino in the knockout stages saw us progress to the final, where we outclassed Auxerre 4-1. The final was televised on a local TV station, and at the start of the match they delivered the ball in a helicopter! It dropped the ball off on the centre spot and flew off again. It was madness and the sort of thing you'd expect to see in American football.

It was a great achievement for us to win the tournament considering the calibre of some of the teams involved and we picked up a host of individual awards too. A lad called John Shotton was man of the match in the final, Mike Pollitt won 'best goalkeeper' and Craig Lawton picked up both top scorer and player of the tournament. It was a big deal for the club to win it and maybe the first sign that the gaffer's investment in the youth system was beginning to pay off. He and Archie Knox met us at Manchester Airport on our return and I've still got a nice photograph of all the lads in our club suits on my wall at home that was taken after we landed. The whole thing had been a great experience, playing against players from different cultures, and to beat four Italian teams on their own soil was massive. Serie A was probably the best league in Europe at that time, so it was a massive statement from United, who still have the trophy in the club's museum, which I'm very proud of.

We were back in FA Youth Cup action at the beginning of January 1990, a trip to Burnley, which we won 4-1 at Turf Moor, with Giggsy getting on the scoresheet. That set up an away tie at Port Vale in the next round, which was the scene of a comfortable 3-0 win and me getting sent off for losing my head. It was a stupid tackle and completely pointless really because we were well in control, with Ryan scoring two more.

I'd never been sent off before and didn't really know what to do with myself. Getting the customary verbals from Eric as I walked past the dugout, I just ended up going to sit in the dressing room with my bottom lip on the floor. I kept my head down when all the lads came in and it probably helped my cause slightly that we'd won.

That incident could form the basis of a humorous pub quiz question: What have Alan Tonge and Paul Pogba got in common? Not a lot, but both of us have been sent off in the FA Youth Cup playing for Manchester United!

Anyway, it meant I was suspended for the next round, a 3-1 win over Sheffield Wednesday, before regaining my place for a home tie with Leicester City, where goals from Craig Lawton and Colin McKee saw us run out 2-0 winners. I picked up an ankle injury though, when I got done late by one of their lads as I was clearing the ball down the line. That kept me out for a few weeks and I got a stern talking to from Eric afterwards in the dressing room about the importance of protecting myself in those sorts of challenges. He said I was too honest trying to clear the ball and reminded me that the sole of your boot was your best friend in football.

I was fit again for the semi-final a month later, which presented us with a difficult draw against Spurs, to be played over two legs. The first was at White Hart Lane, which was an exciting prospect as it meant travelling down the day before and staying in a hotel. I think Spurs had knocked Manchester City out in the previous round, which a few of the lads, including Eric, went to watch. There was a lot of noise about their left-winger Scott Houghton, who I'd be marking, and how quick he was. They weren't wrong, to be fair, as he was very good at drawing you in before taking the ball past you, so I tried to do him early and took the resultant booking. It was high, and reports describe it as a 'dangerous challenge', which was true because I think I hit him in the chest with my studs.

It didn't stop him, unfortunately, and he scored just after half-time to make it 1-0. They added a second from a counter-attack just a few minutes later to give us a mountain to climb back at Old Trafford. I remember Eric hammering Sean McAuley afterwards for switching off.

We gave it a real go in the second leg and were straight out of the blocks. Adrian Doherty put us one up with a decent goal where he got away from his marker and swept the ball home. The Old Trafford crowd roared us on. We had plenty of chances and I remember Giggsy hitting the post. Sadly, they scored a late equaliser to take it away from us. It just wasn't our night. Maybe if luck had smiled on us a bit more we might have got to the final. So near, yet so far. Eric Harrison was naturally disappointed afterwards but I remember him saying we'd been fantastic and they couldn't ask any more of us.

So that was my FA Youth Cup experience with United: a quarter-final and a semi-final. You could see progress was being made and the lads got to the semi-final again in 1990/91 before the fabled Class of '92 came along the year after. Things take time but the club got it right in the end.

Our group were knocking on the door but just fell short with fine margins. It makes you wonder what would have happened if we'd managed to win the FA Youth Cup that season because we'd already won the Grossi-Morera plus the Lancashire League with the 'A' team, which we did three years on the bounce. You may have never heard of the Class of '92!

You look at the players in that group and obviously Giggsy is the anomaly with the amazing career he had, but of the rest of us only Darren Ferguson, Mark Bosnich (over two spells), Ian Wilkinson and Colin McKee played competitive matches in the first team. It just wasn't the right time to bring a load of young players through like it was a few years later when the stars aligned because the first team were struggling, so it ended up being a bit of a forgotten era. I look back at that group of players and what we achieved with a lot of pride but also a touch of sadness that a lot of us weren't able to progress.

If you take the group of lads I was signed with just after Fergie took over, all of whom were in and around that youth team, none of us made a competitive first-team appearance for the club due to various factors, although a few of us did manage to have careers in professional football with varying degrees of success.

Micky Pollitt was probably the most successful. I'd known Mick since we were 11 or 12, playing grassroots football for Moss Bank in Bolton. He was a real character, like a lot of goalkeepers tend to be, but in a nice way, and he loved the banter. I think he found it quite difficult at United, as there was fierce competition for places in every position, but the club were particularly well stocked in the goalkeeping department, meaning he struggled to progress. He featured in the disastrous FA Youth Cup defeat to Mansfield Town at just 15 and I remember him telling me that he'd been really nervous. It would have been a tough experience. Apprentice numbers in the years immediately before our crop were pretty low and there were only a handful of lads in the year above us. They struggled for strength in depth, which often resulted in younger lads being roped in who maybe weren't ready to play at that level.

I think Mick realised that he needed to look elsewhere for opportunities and he went on to have an unbelievable career that included spells at Lincoln City, Rotherham United, Chesterfield and Wigan Athletic, where he was part of the team that won the FA Cup in 2012/13. He was still playing well into his 40s and is now goalkeeping coach at Preston North End. I saw him a few years ago and I remember him saying he felt he'd been so lucky because he'd never had to come out of football – fair play to him.

Jason Lydiate was a big centre-half from Salford who was quite mature and developed for his age so found himself a regular in the reserves quite quickly. He was reliable, good in the air and a powerful header of the ball who could also play. I'd often play next to him at right-back or centre-half and we had a good understanding. I think if he'd got an opportunity in the first team he wouldn't have let you down, but sadly it never came because he had Gary Pallister and Steve Bruce in front of him. It's difficult to blood a young lad in that position, especially in those days when most centre-forwards were proper hard cases. Jason played a decent number of games in the Football League after leaving United, most notably for Bolton Wanderers and Blackpool, and is now coaching, I believe.

Paul Sixsmith was a left-back or left-sided player who I'd also known since playing kids' football in Bolton. He was tricky, like an Arnold Mühren style of player in that he wasn't the quickest but had a wand of a left foot. His career took a rather interesting path as he went out to play in Malta, where he met his wife, and is still there as far as I know. He even gained citizenship and won caps for their national team.

Kieran Toal was a really talented player who played quite a few friendlies for the first team. He was a clever lad who was very academic, and an intelligent footballer too, with a great touch. A good header of the ball, he could really leap and hang there a bit like Cristiano Ronaldo. When I bumped into Fergie at an ex-players' do a few years ago he said that Kieran's dad used to continuously say he was going to be the greatest player ever!

His football career ended up being quite short, although I believe he did feature for the Republic of Ireland at youth level. He was released just after United won the Premier League at the end of 1992/93 and drifted out of the game after a brief spell with Motherwell. He's now a big-hitter in the law industry, so investing in his education and having that broader identity paid off for him in the long term.

Chris Taylor was a bit of a sad one. He was probably one of the most talented players in our group and a little bit like Robin Van Persie, with a very dominant left foot. At the age of about 15 he was absolutely flying but tragically lost his dad young and wasn't able to continue that progression. He probably should have been supported better by the club but it just wasn't the right time in his life for it all to click into place and he lost a lot of confidence. I'd love to know what he's doing now because I've never heard from him since we were at United.

Despite our long-term prospects, success in the Youth Cup was almost used as a way of judging a group of young players, and given we'd done quite well United offered professional contracts to a few of us when our YTS deals expired in the summer of 1990, including myself, Mick, Kieran, Jason and Paul. They offered me a one-year deal on £150 a week, take it or leave it, so obviously, being United daft, I took it. There were no agents in those days to represent you or try to negotiate a better deal. They literally just called you into the gaffer's office and he'd deliver the verdict as to whether you were being kept on or let go.

There were a few perks to go with the pay rise, including a promotion of sorts into the reserve-team dressing room and having the pleasure of someone cleaning my boots. John Sharples, who was only the year below, used to do them for me. They used to call him 'the mad dog' because he was everywhere on the pitch, and a good lad.

It had been an eventful couple of years with plenty of ups and downs but ultimately I'd achieved my goal of becoming a professional footballer at Manchester United. I came out of my contract meeting absolutely buzzing, but this is where football starts to get a bit grey because nobody really talks about what deal they've been given. Then you start to hear whispers that other lads have been given two- or even three-year deals and you begin to wonder why you're down the pecking order ...

Chapter 10

She Wore a Scarlet Ribbon

THERE WAS a lot of tension around the club during the 1989/90 season. The first team weren't doing well in the league, eventually finishing a lowly 13th, and the fans were becoming impatient with the manager. At one match a lad called Pete Molyneux even held up a banner that read, '3 years of excuses and it's still crap, ta ra Fergie', which given what unfolded over the next 23 years has gone down in history.

The FA Cup offered some salvation and the chance for the club to win its first trophy in five years. They say a Mark Robins goal in the third round against Nottingham Forest saved the gaffer's job; I'm not sure how true that is but it was probably getting close.

A 1-0 win against Hereford in the fourth round set up a tie at Newcastle, which they took me along for, to help out with the kit. That was an interesting experience as it meant being around the first team again even if I wasn't going to be involved in the match itself. I had to help get the skip off the bus, unload it and tidy everything up afterwards.

The match was very end to end in front of a hostile Geordie crowd, and at half-time I sat awkwardly in the corner of the dressing room while the gaffer absolutely ranted and raved. He gave a player the full hairdryer treatment and actually hung him up by the back of his shirt on the peg where he'd got changed. It was absolutely surreal and not for the first time I remember wondering whether professional football was the right fit for me.

Luckily, Danny Wallace ended up scoring a nice goal to help us seal a 3-2 victory and we started to gain a bit of momentum after that with another 1-0 win at Sheffield United seeing us through to the semi-finals. Oldham Athletic were the opponents and were a very good team in those days, with the likes of Andy Ritchie, Denis Irwin, Ian Marshall, Gunnar Halle and Earl Barrett in their squad. The tie was played at Maine Road and was an incredible spectacle that finished 3-3 but Mark Robins scored the winner in the replay to take us to Wembley.

The build-up to the final against Crystal Palace was exciting at a time when cup finals were still cup finals rather than the diluted version you get these days. As you'd expect there was a big clamour for tickets and all the apprentices were given six each. That meant suddenly everyone was your best mate and I remember getting a phone call at home from a lad who I hadn't spoken to for about five years to see whether I could sort him out. I ended up giving all mine to family or away for face value but a few of the other lads saw a business opportunity and managed to flog theirs to make a small fortune. You could see the temptation given the modest wages we were on and I remember one of the lads sticking a massive wad of cash into his blazer, which must have amounted to a couple of grand. It was allowed to happen and most of the first team were at it too, to be fair.

United took all the players and staff down to Wembley, where we stayed in a big hotel before going to the game all smartly dressed in our club suits. We were really looked after and made to feel part of it on what was a special occasion. I took my first girlfriend with me and it's a great memory to have. It was my first visit to the Mecca of football, and the old Wembley was such a historic venue with its twin towers. In truth, the place was probably a little tired by then and, looking back, wasn't what you'd call a state-of-the-art facility. You imagined it as being really grand but in reality it was actually quite grey and things such as the seats weren't the best. It's had an upgrade since then though. I've taught in a classroom that overlooks the new one, which is a lot fresher, and the arch over it is impressive.

The final itself was an interesting one in front of a passionate crowd. United fans were out in full force, and the Palace end was packed with a mass of red and blue balloons. Palace were a decent team who had beaten Liverpool in the other semi-final and probably deserved to win on the day because they had us on the rack a couple of times. Ian Wright scored twice and it looked like they'd done us but Mark Hughes grabbed a late equaliser in extra time to force another replay, so we were back at Wembley the following Thursday.

The big story before the second match was the manager choosing to drop his goalkeeper Jim Leighton, who was probably at fault for a couple of goals in the first contest. It was a big shock and a massive call to make because Jim had played most fixtures that season and been Fergie's goalkeeper up at Aberdeen. He was a quiet bloke who didn't say much and it finished him at United. His relationship with the gaffer broke down completely after that and I don't think they've spoken since.

His replacement Les Sealey was the polar opposite; they were like chalk and cheese. Fergie has said since in one of his books that Les wasn't a better goalkeeper than Jim but Les thought he was, and that kind of confidence can make the difference in a match as big as a cup final. They say Jim is still bitter about it to this day but, ultimately, as harsh as it was, it proved to be the right decision.

That night also left fond memories for Lee Martin, who was the surprising hero, scoring the only goal for United to lift the cup. We'd had a bit of luck along the way, which you often need, and it was sheer jubilation on the final whistle. It was a special night and a massive buzz for the club to finally win a trophy after a difficult few years. Those lads were my heroes and it was an absolute privilege to learn from them and see how they operated on a daily basis. They weren't just brilliant footballers but great people too, and here are a few memories of each of them.

Les Sealey

A proper character and that's putting it mildly – he was bonkers! Les was a bit of a wheeler and dealer who would fit the description of a flash cockney. He was always on his mobile phone, which were in their infancy back in 1990 so it was the size of a brick. I think he had a car sales business on the side and was a bit like the assistant manager in *Mike Bassett*, trying to flog cars to players in his spare time. That'll be the Daewoo!

I played alongside him on a couple of occasions and he was a very vocal keeper who would be barking out instructions to his defence. Like a lot of goalkeepers he absolutely detested getting chipped in training and would go berserk if anyone dared to do it, usually chasing them across the pitch while the rest of us looked on laughing.

He was a cult hero with the fans because he played in some important matches for the club at the start of its resurgence, staying in the team after the cup final until Peter Schmeichel arrived a year later. He was a good man who died young, which was really sad, but he left plenty of fond memories.

Mike Phelan

Mick was and still is a very humble guy. As a footballer he was more solid and reliable as opposed to spectacular but he made a great career out of it. A good player to have in any squad, he didn't possess great pace but was an extremely good passer of the ball.

He scored a cracking goal for Norwich City at Old Trafford prior to signing for United and when I've bumped into him in recent times still jokes that Fergie signed him on that alone! Towards the end of his career, they kept him around to help the young players in the reserves because he was a rock-solid pro and I'm not surprised that he went on to play a massive role at the club as a coach. A very steady player and a top-class bloke.

Steve Bruce

What always struck me with Brucey was that he was hard as nails, with a confidence about him. He had a strong personality and was a leader who was very vocal, talking players around in the back four in his Geordie accent. I was fortunate enough to play alongside him a couple of times in the reserves and the Histon friendly.

You wouldn't mess with him and he had a presence, like the time he had young Stevie Carter by the scruff of his neck at The Cliff. Overall, Brucey had a fantastic career before going into management.

Gary Pallister

Pally was a nice fella and laid-back character who was often the target of the gaffer's hairdryer as his record signing at the time.

He could take it though, and was maybe a good foil for Fergie to vent at.

He got caught on his heels a couple of times in the first match of that cup final and sometimes struggled to turn quickly because he was such a big lad who tended to find it difficult against small, nippy players. He was quick when he got into his stride though. A classy player who became a top servant.

Lee Martin

A lovely lad who's only a couple of years older than me, Lee was a good player who was two-footed and could play on either side. We were all buzzing for him when he got the winner in the replay, and although he played a decent number of times for the first team I think his only other goal was a deflection against West Ham.

I still see him at the ex-players' do's. He's a humble fella who had his challenges coming out of football but not many people can say they've scored the winning goal for Manchester United in an FA Cup Final, and he's quite rightly very proud of it.

Neil Webb

Webby's United career was an interesting one. He signed from Nottingham Forest as an England international with a big reputation but it didn't quite happen for him.

I remember him being unbelievable on his debut, a 4-1 win over Arsenal on the opening day of that 1989/90 season, which is memorable for Michael Knighton running on to the pitch juggling the ball, as he was in talks to buy the club. Neil was a nice person to speak to, with no airs or graces, but was unfortunate to suffer a bad Achilles injury while at the club and at times seemed a little weighty. Last I heard of him after his retirement from football is that he works for the Royal Mail as a postman.

Paul Ince

Incey was a very good player who had pace and the ability to drive forward from midfield. He used to call me 'Tonga' and I liked him even though he was an extrovert and had plenty to say for himself.

I'm not too sure how he sits in United fans' opinions because he did the unthinkable and signed for Liverpool later in his career. He was one of the established players sacrificed by Fergie in the summer of 1995 when the Class of '92 were coming through, along with Andrei Kanchelskis and Mark Hughes, so maybe he was bitter about that, but time helps to forgive.

He was a brilliant player for the club though, who was absolutely top class for a few seasons and an important member of the 1992/93 team that won the Premier League title after a 26-year wait.

Bryan Robson

Captain Marvel. Robbo was the main man and he was just brilliant. The best.

There aren't many players in history who you could describe as an all-round footballer; they say Duncan Edwards had it, and Bryan Robson definitely did too. He was a colossus who could get up and down the pitch, pass, head the ball, lead a team and score goals. For many years United were a poorer team when he didn't play, which speaks volumes. He just had everything, and to top it off he was a brilliant bloke who always had time for us youngsters.

Danny Wallace

Danny had come through at Southampton with his brothers Rod and Ray before they'd all splintered off and gone their separate ways. I played a couple of times with him in the 'A' team and remember him as a quiet lad who was reserved.

On the pitch he was very quick, with a low centre of gravity, and he had his moments for United, scoring at Newcastle as part of that cup run and in the semi-final against Oldham. His career ended prematurely due to the onset of multiple sclerosis, which was a real shame.

Brian McClair

Choccy mostly kept himself to himself. He was quiet but had a good sense of humour. He could be very cutting and kill you with a one-liner in his thick Scottish accent.

Brian had a cracking career with United, and Celtic before that. He could score goals and I think Fergie put a lot of faith in him. He wasn't your typical footballer as he struck me as an educated lad with other interests outside the game, often writing things for the matchday programme. He's got his own podcast these days, which is really popular.

Mark Hughes

I remember going to Old Trafford for a medical at the start of my YTS deal with United in the summer of 1988, which was the same day Sparky was being unveiled as having re-signed for the club. I can vaguely recall seeing him being photographed in the stands or maybe on the pitch with the scarf, and his Porsche was in the car park. A few of the lads had their picture taken with it.

He was hard as nails on-field but very quiet off it, almost like two different characters that switched places every time he set foot on a football pitch. A brilliant centre-forward.

Clayton Blackmore

Clayton was a very underrated player who could strike the ball brilliantly and play in several different positions. I think I read somewhere he played in all the shirt numbers for United bar goalkeeper. A handsome lad who got christened 'Sunbed' because he was always tanned and well groomed. He was just a nice, reserved bloke who loved playing football, and I had a few matches with him in the reserves.

He's a very good golfer and still shows his face from time to time at ex-players' dinners and events.

Mark Robins

Mark was a very good goalscorer at youth and reserve level and he bagged a few for the first team as well. He was a very fit lad and always led the cross-country runs. He has had a very successful career in management since he finished playing. At the time of writing, he's the gaffer at Coventry City, where he's done a magnificent job, and he'll always be remembered for scoring the all-important goal in the third round that they say saved Fergie's bacon.

* * *

Manchester United were on the up and there was a sense that the club was finally beginning to turn a corner. Winning that FA Cup gave the gaffer a bit of room to breathe and he never looked back after that. Joining in with the celebrations, having recently been awarded a professional contract, the future felt bright and I was thrilled to be a part of it.

I went away to Malia that summer with my girlfriend, while the Italia 90 World Cup was on. I admired a lot of the England team and had seen most of them play in the flesh when they visited Old Trafford with their respective teams – the likes of Paul Gascoigne, Gary Lineker, Paul Parker and Des Walker were great players who I loved studying.

I was in a bar when former United apprentice David Platt scored his famous swivel volley against Belgium in extra time with the match heading to penalties. The place went mental and everyone jumped in the pool! I was still out there for the match against Cameroon, who had us on the ropes. They were a bit of an unknown quantity but played some great stuff, and we maybe got away with one.

I was back home for the semi-final and penalty heartbreak against West Germany, commonly remembered for Gazza's tears after being booked, which meant he couldn't have played in the final had we got there. It's maybe such an iconic moment because at that time it wasn't common for footballers or men in general to show their emotions. Any sign of sensitivity was seen as a weakness that could be targeted and you were just expected to get on with it.

When you look back at it, 1990 was a big year on many fronts, including my 18th birthday, among other things. United had won the first of many trophies under Fergie and Liverpool their last league title for 30 years, so the balance of power was beginning to shift. In boxing the seemingly invincible 'Iron' Mike Tyson lost his world heavyweight championship belt to Buster Douglas in a huge upset that sent shockwaves across the globe. Nelson Mandela was released from prison in South Africa and, in the

UK, Margaret Thatcher's controversial tenure as Prime Minister was ended. Manchester as a city was beginning to explode with the Hacienda nightclub in its pomp and a vibrant music scene with local bands such as the Happy Mondays and Stone Roses achieving worldwide acclaim.

The world was changing and football was changing too, with the advent of the Premier League just a few years away. Having recently achieved my ambition of becoming a professional footballer, I was hopeful of a long career in the game.

Chapter 11

Fergie

'NO FUCKING chance. Close the door on your way out!'

I was a first-year pro earning £150 a week and a few of the lads around the first team had been cheekily encouraging us to ask the gaffer for a pay rise. I went in and asked for an extra £20; he just looked at me across his desk and told me to get out!

Alex Ferguson had arrived at Manchester United in November 1986 having achieved great things up at Aberdeen, but success hadn't really been forthcoming, and the late 80s generally wasn't the best time. There were no trophies and we were struggling, which meant the manager was often very angry or volatile because he was under pressure to bring success back to the club. He arrived with Archie Knox as his assistant and usually within football management duos there's a bad cop and a good cop. Fergie was a bad cop and Archie was an even badder cop! He could cut you down in front of others without batting an eyelid. I remember him brutally telling a youth player who had miscontrolled the ball that he had a touch like 'an epileptic camel'.

On a Saturday afternoon I'd usually go to the match at Old Trafford with my dad and brother, making use of my two complimentary tickets, and I could get in with my player's pass.

The football in Fergie's early days wasn't the best and we finished well down the league on a few occasions. We were runners-up in 1987/88 behind Liverpool but dipped again the following season. There were a few players who were maybe a bit lightweight and I think the gaffer knew he needed more strength in his team as we were decent on our day but lacked consistency and seemed to fall short when it mattered. Teams such as Derby County were coming to Old Trafford and winning on a regular basis. The United team and manager were booed off a lot, and if things had worked out slightly differently the club could have let him go.

I remember seeing Bill Foulkes outside the ground after one match and him stopping to talk to my dad: 'Wasn't the best today, Bill.'

'Oh, it's grim, isn't it.' That was coming from a Busby Babe who had played hundreds of times for United, so goes to show the level of feeling in those years, and it echoed throughout the club. There was a lot of uncertainty and fractures that took time to correct. The gaffer was laying the foundations but the culture still wasn't quite right, so everything was a bit disjointed. The FA Cup win in 1990 was golden for him because it bought him more time.

He wanted to go back to the club's ethos of producing its own players, like in the days of Sir Matt Busby, and a few lads did get chances in the first team. The likes of Russell Beardsmore, Jules Maiorana, Derek Brazil, Tony Gill, Lee Martin and David Wilson, to name a few, all shone for a while but weren't really long-lasting because it's easier for young players to be eased into a team that's winning.

The Class of '92 came along a few years later when things were going a bit better, and the belief in that group was unbelievable. I don't think their success as a collective will ever be repeated because times are different now, but those players formed the backbone of the team that won countless trophies over the next two decades.

Alex's son Darren was also in and around the first team and was still at the club when United first won the Premier League title in 1992/93, even playing enough times to qualify for a medal. I got on well with Darren, who was a top lad and a very decent player, but if I'm being honest there were other lads that were just as good if not better who never got a chance. He was in an awkward situation but would often trigger resentment from the other lads when he'd be excused early from the jobs we had to do as apprentices so he could get a lift home with his dad, which undermined the whole notion and ethic that we were all in it together.

To be fair to him, he went on to carve a decent career for himself in the Football League with Wolves then Wrexham before moving into management, and even today a few appearances in United's first team can build a pedigree for players that allows them to get good moves further down the line. His brother Jason also played a few matches in United's youth teams before drifting away, but Darren was the better player of the two.

The gaffer was more of a background figure in my time at the club. You were aware of his presence but he'd just be keeping an eye on stuff. He was a good observer, as were the likes of Eric Harrison and Kiddo, because they were watching you all the time. It was like a late 80s version of *Big Brother* where nothing went unnoticed.

I can't remember him taking a lot of training sessions, to be honest. He'd maybe come over and do some finishing work with us, where he could blow up if you mishit the ball or made an error. He'd be testing you to see how you reacted. If you can't take it in a situation like that, how are you going to cope in a hostile environment like Anfield or Highbury?

He'd sometimes join in with the small-sided games at The Cliff but wasn't the best player. He was pretty awful to be honest. His fitness seemed fine but his touch was questionable. On many occasions his second touch was a tackle. Nobby Stiles and Kiddo would occasionally take part and they still had their technical ability and quality, but Fergie was bang average at best and you wouldn't have guessed that he'd been a decent pro in Scotland. If he was on your team, you were carrying him. It was tough because you couldn't have a go at him and it was never his fault if things weren't going well, unsurprisingly. He wasn't slow to let you know if you weren't up to standard though, so it was hard work.

He'd often have a few of us stay behind after training to play head tennis in the gym. He might have had a match to go to in the evening, and that was his way of killing time in the afternoon. It used to go on for hours sometimes or until he and Archie Knox won. They'd make one of the apprentices officiate, which was an unenviable task to say the least. Let's just say that he could have given John McEnroe a run for his money! He was so competitive and everything was based around winning. He could become volatile and lose his temper a lot and would sometimes go nose to nose with players.

Looking back, he was under a lot of pressure, which manifests itself in different ways, but I think that's how the 'hairdryer' was born and it wasn't nice to be on the receiving end. I never got it directly from him but I saw it in action a few times. We played a Lancashire Youth Cup semi-final on Old Trafford against Manchester City one year on a sunny evening towards the end of the season. He was determined that the club's scouting and youth system was going to overtake theirs but we were 2-0 down at half-time and ended up losing 3-1. Afterwards he almost smashed the dressing room door off its hinges. He went mad, and a little Welsh midfielder called Lee Costa got torn to shreds. The gaffer would clench his fists behind him and was shouting about an inch away from Lee's nose. It was nasty and not pleasant to witness: 'YOU ARE FUCKING USELESS AND AN ABSOLUTE EMBARRASSMENT! YOU BETTER START LOOKING FOR ANOTHER FUCKING CLUB!'

He was a man on a mission. I'd started training with the club in the later days of Ron Atkinson but never really came across him. He sounded a lot more player-friendly, whereas Alex was more about discipline. He was the change agent for the club and had the pedigree to arrive at United and try to do things differently.

I think he had a bit of a chip on his shoulder about the way his own playing career had turned out and that's what drove him to be successful in management. He wasn't treated well at his boyhood club Rangers and was blamed for Billy McNeill's goal for Celtic in a Scottish Cup Final. He probably carried a bitterness about that, which drove him. It set something in motion that started at Aberdeen and carried on at United, although it took time to get going with the latter.

He was tough but fair and had a sense of humour. You always used to hear him singing to himself as he wandered down the corridors at The Cliff when he was in a good mood and he used to have like a nervous cough to clear his throat, which meant you could usually hear him coming. As an apprentice that was the time to look busy and not be caught messing about. He had a big presence and you sensed that he ruled with an iron rod, like a Mafia boss or a school headteacher, because there was no mistaking who was number one at that club.

He could also be a bit of a wind-up merchant too. There were two ladies who worked in the canteen at The Cliff, Theresa and Gail, who were both lovely but got wound up mercilessly. I remember one of them knocked a cone over as they were driving across the car park so Fergie called her from the phone in his office pretending to be the police while she was on the payphone at the top of the stairs. 'It's Greater Manchester police speaking. You've killed a cone and unfortunately we're going to have to come down and arrest you.' Poor Theresa or Gail fell for it and panicked. He found stuff like that terribly funny.

I was well-behaved and never really gave him a problem but we only had a distant relationship. I was quite reserved, which probably counted against me because he'd have been looking towards the more established players rather than a shy, sensitive young lad who gave his all. Managers often favour players who they see a bit of themselves in and I don't think he'd have got that from me, unfortunately.

Other lads did step out of line and got on the wrong side of him. I remember Mike Pollitt was a massive Bolton fan and they had a big match in the FA Cup so he phoned in sick on the Saturday morning when he was supposed to be playing for the 'B' team. He was actually going to watch the match and still recalls walking across the forecourt at Burnden Park before kick-off and to his horror bumping into Archie Knox and the gaffer coming the other way! Mick told me the gaffer remembered it straight away when he went back to Old Trafford in his Wigan Athletic days, nearly a quarter of a century later.

He'd often come to watch the youth team on a Saturday morning and you could feel his presence on the touchline. He'd be chatting to the parents with Archie Knox and would watch a bit before drifting away to prepare for the first-team match that afternoon. You didn't want to make a mistake while he was there and you could feel everyone raising their game to catch his eye. Some lads only turned it on when Alex and Archie were watching, which was very frustrating because its fine margins, and these are the people you want to impress as a young player, as they are, arguably, the gatekeepers to you having a career.

The gaffer had an outstanding level of attention to detail and knew everything about everybody. He had encyclopaedic knowledge and would retain every little detail about everyone connected with the club. He'd often ask me how my dad was getting on at British Gas, which was amazing considering the number of people he was dealing with.

Like a lot of Manchester United managers, he was well-informed and fans would let him know if one of his players was coming out of a nightclub at half two in the morning. Players had to be careful because he'd put them on the spot and spring stuff on them that they didn't know he knew. He benefitted from being in a position where he could achieve near absolute control because players weren't as powerful as they are now. The wages weren't as high and the Premier League was still a few years off.

I think he mellowed after I left, when the success started to come, and it's amazing how he adapted because the game had completely changed by the time he retired in 2013. In more recent times I've bumped into him at reunions and former players' dinners where we've had a couple of nice interactions.

I won a photograph of Denis Law in a raffle at one a few years ago, and the gaffer was on the top table. The compere said, 'We've got Alan Tonge coming up. Sir Alex's first signing, I believe.' That got a clap from the audience as I went up to collect my prize. At another I remember him saying to my son Sam, in a tongue-in-cheek manner, 'I hope you're a better player than your dad was.'

It was funny; you almost feel 18 again when you're in front of him and he's still very sharp. Even though three whole decades have passed since he was my boss it's good to know that you're never forgotten.

I do think that he perhaps tries to forget about his early days at the club when I was there because they're not fond memories for him compared to the years that followed and all the trophies. He's probably the greatest manager of all time and that's the esteem he's held in. I'm just proud to have played a very small part in the story.

Chapter 12

Don't Look Back in Anger

THE 1990/91 season at Manchester United was much more promising than the ones that had gone before. The FA Cup win the previous season provided the springboard for the first team to finish sixth in the league, which was a marked improvement. There was also a Rumbelows Cup Final appearance at Wembley, where Sheffield Wednesday got the better of us 1-0 and, of course, the 2-1 European Cup Winners' Cup win over Barcelona in Rotterdam.

The foundations for what would make the club so successful over the next two decades were starting to fall into place. The lads who would become known as the Class of '92 were starting to appear around The Cliff and in the junior teams. I'm sure I shooed a young spiky-haired David Beckham out of our dressing room on at least one occasion, recognising him from a picture in the club programme advertising Bobby Charlton's soccer schools. I also remember seeing Gary Neville turn up in a cricket jumper. He and his brother Phil were both decent cricketers in their youth so it makes sense now because he might have come straight from a game, but I didn't know that at the time. I just thought he was odd. Then there was Robbie Savage, who was very quiet and didn't say much – you can't shut him up now!

I was there on Andrei Kanchelskis's first day, when we played a practice match in which he was unbelievable. Paul Sixsmith was playing left-back and Andrei just turned him inside out. He ran riot a few times in training sessions on Littleton Road too. He was very direct and a proper old-fashioned winger, so it was easy to see why he became a fans' favourite who scored some cracking goals. He hit the ground running too, which you don't always see nowadays with some players needing 12 or 18 months to adapt to the demands of the Premier League. At the time you didn't really get a lot of lads coming over from the continent so it can't have been easy for him trying to settle into a completely different culture with a language barrier to overcome.

I spent most of that season, my first as a pro, in the 'A' team, where I played pretty much every match, with a handful of ressies appearances thrown in, so looking back I wasn't exactly breaking the door down to be included in the first-team squad. At the time, though, you don't see what's coming and are just sleepwalking towards your contract meeting at the end of the season.

The last few weeks were pretty frantic for the 'A' team that year as we were going for the league title. Bad weather over the winter meant that we ended up with a backlog of four matches in the space of a week, which included fixtures at Burnley and Morecambe to set up a title decider against Manchester City's 'A' team at Platt Lane. I think we were level on points going into it but goals from Giggsy and Colin McKee saw us over the line with a 2-1 victory. I've still got the newspaper clipping with the team line-up, and it was a decent one, with Mark Bosnich, Deiniol Graham and John O'Kane also featuring.

John was a really talented youngster who would have still been at school at that stage but was deemed good enough to mix it with lads who were two or three years older. He was another whose personality didn't really fit the culture of the club but went on to be part of the Class of '92 team that won the FA Youth Cup the following season and played a few times in United's first team before getting a move to Everton. In recent times he's released his own book, entitled *Bursting the Bubble: Football, Autism and Me*, which is an honest account of his career in football while being on the autistic spectrum. I'm very proud of John for opening up and speaking his truth.

We were all buzzing afterwards and I remember Fergie coming into the changing room and giving out loads of praise. I'd been up against a lad called Jason Beckford, who had already played in City's first team, and I managed to keep him quiet all match: 'Brilliant today, Tongey lad. You handled Beckford really well. Absolutely fantastic, son.' You're always looking for clues as to whether the coaches rate you or not and, knowing my contract was up at the end of the season, I remember sitting there thinking, *I'm going to be alright then.*

It proved to be false hope. A few days later I was in the dressing room at The Cliff getting ready to go out and train when Brian Whitehouse stuck his head round the door. 'Right Al, come with me.' I was watching his facial expression and body language to try to gauge what was to come as we went up the stairs to the gaffer's office but didn't really get anything back.

I knocked on the door. 'Alan Tonge to see you, gaffer.'

I sat down and Fergie didn't beat about the bush. 'It's bad news, son. We're not going to renew your contract. We think you lack a yard of pace to make it as a first-team player here.'

Your whole body just sinks and crumples in on itself like a boxer who's just suffered a devastating knockout they didn't see coming. In an instant my world had come crashing down. It's one of those moments in your life when time stands still and you attempt to fully digest what you've just been told. I was absolutely gutted and just remember thanking him for the opportunity to play for such a great club. I was in a haze and didn't know what to do with myself. I felt like I'd let people down, and the thought of telling my mum and dad when I got home was almost unbearable.

They still made me go out to train that morning and, unsurprisingly, I was all over the place. It was the last place I wanted to be, running round Littleton Road with tears streaming down my face. Paul Ince had a right go at me after I took a heavy touch in the five-a-side match we were playing but my head was completely elsewhere.

I honestly wouldn't wish it on anyone. Deselection at that time in football was ruthless and there was no emotional support or aftercare departments, which have only recently started to appear within academies. You were just discarded like an empty crisp packet. Football is unforgiving and very cruel, with a lot of players within the system being set up to fail. Coaches can string you along, and the sad fact is some players in a youth team are just there to fill a spot so that the likes of Giggsy can progress with the red carpet already rolled out for them. Every kid in that position has blinkers on and thinks their chance will come. You have to, in a way, and you become so engrossed in it, but it's like an illusion, the oasis in the desert, because in hindsight the writing was on the wall.

Youth football is just a cattle market, and if you're a talented player at the age of about 16 you've got a pound sign on your back because you could be worth something to someone. The brutal reality of elite-level sport is you're just an object, which probably explains why so many players released from academies experience personal problems or mental health issues. You come away from it feeling used, and you've made a lot of sacrifices to get there, like not going out with your mates, weekends and even birthdays sometimes. Those experiences that normal teenage lads can crack on and enjoy, for what? You have to face up to your family, knowing you've been bombed out, and find the character to keep going with your life, but it's not easy.

It was a really tough period for me, especially from a well-being perspective, because I was trying to come to terms with the fact that my dream had been shattered. It was hard enough but then you've also got to deal with being the subject of the inevitable gossip. As a young footballer there can be a bit of jealousy and people are quick to tear you down. I remember sitting round a table in a pub with my girlfriend and some of her friends when one of their partners asked why I'd been sacked by United! I had to correct them and explain that I hadn't done anything wrong, they just weren't renewing my contract.

Looking back at it all now I never felt I had the confidence and trust of the coaching staff at United, which you need really because managers can make or break careers. Time and patience also don't exist in football. I wasn't the type to go knocking on the gaffer's door if I had any issues in my life because I'd just speak to my parents. Maybe that's what I should have been doing at 17, to ask what I needed to do to get into the first team. You're only asking a question but at the time it seemed so daunting.

Like a lot of the other lads, the environment wasn't right for me to thrive in and my reserved personality didn't really suit the culture. I was at United for about five years but during that time I never truly felt I fitted in there, which was a heartbreaking realisation, having loved the club since I was a child. It was like being invisible at times. I think Eric Cantona said that everything has to be right in order for a club to be successful – the manager, the players, the culture, and if it had been in a better place I might have stood more chance of fulfilling my potential.

I think even my adaptability and versatility counted against me. I could turn my hand to a few different positions but that's not always a good thing because it stops you from being allowed to settle and grow into a particular spot. I was shunted about a bit.

It would have meant everything for me to have played a few or even just one competitive match for the first team but there was so much competition. The likes of Viv Anderson, Denis Irwin, Lee Martin, Clayton Blackmore and Paul Ince could all play in my position and were well established. How do you compete with that? You need to be a really good player to even get in the door at United, which I'm very proud of, but it can feel like you didn't quite achieve your ambitions after getting so close. Maybe I'm being too harsh on myself. Fans often say to me, 'You lived the dream,' but I'd say that some of the more negative experiences I had there had a lasting impact as I moved through life. It was a classic case of wrong place, wrong time, but if I hadn't had that experience would my life have taken the course it ended up doing? Maybe not.

I had to accept it was all coming to an end. It was over and my relationship with United had completely broken down. I played one of my last matches for the club in the reserves towards the end of the season, on the left wing against Sheffield United at Bramall Lane, which was strange considering I was a right-back or centre-half. Looking back now I was just there to make up the numbers. If they were trying to put me in the shop window, then playing me out of position wasn't going to help my situation. I was up against Chris Wilder that night and remember hitting the post, which wasn't bad considering I hadn't played there since I was about 14.

I loved United and still do. It's my club. I remember towards the end some of the other lads who were being released were nicking bits of kit and taking what they could get from the club after it had disposed of them. I couldn't bring myself to do it. In my eyes that was Manchester United's kit and it was stealing. I wasn't going to disrespect the club in that way, even if some of my experiences there could have been better.

It's like some relationships in life. If someone has treated you badly but you love them enough, you almost have to shed that, push it to one side and try to move on. My love for the club will never change and I often think a football fan's relationship with their team can be complicated or even difficult at times, especially if you've been lucky enough to play for them.

Right from an early age I always seemed to have a ball at my feet and life revolved around football.

I loved playing for my grassroots team Bolton Lads Club and a few of us went on to play professionally. Here we are after winning another trophy.

The Manchester United squad photo 1988/89. To be sat alongside those players was an absolute dream come true.

Sat behind Alex Ferguson and Bryan Robson at Old Trafford. I hope they weren't talking about me!

A great honour to be named captain of a Football League XI celebrating a centenary against our Russian counterparts at the Luzhniki Stadium in Moscow.

Arriving back at Manchester Airport after winning the Grossi Morera youth tournament in Italy. We picked up a host of individual awards too and cleaned up!

the
MANCHESTER UNITED
FOOTBALL CLUB plc
OLD TRAFFORD
MANCHESTER M16 0RA
Registered Office: Old Trafford, Manchester, M16 0RA

Registered No. 95489 England
Telephone:
061-872 1661 (Office)
061-872 0199 (Ticket and
Match Enquiries)
061-872 3488 (Commercial
Department)
Fax No: 061-873 7210
Telex: 666564 United G

Chief Executive	Manager	Secretary	Commercial Manager
C. Martin Edwards	Alex Ferguson	Kenneth R. Merrett	D. A. McGregor

KRM/LL

16 May 1990

Mr A Tonge
3 Lincoln Avenue
Little Lever,
Lancs

Dear Alan,

I write to inform you that your Trainee Contract expires on
the 30th June 1990, and we have pleasure in advising you
that a Contract will be offered on the following terms:

ONE YEAR

1/7/90-30/6/91   £150.   Per week.

£100. Appearance. (First Team)

I would be obliged if you would advise me as soon as
possible if you accept these terms. A stamped addressed
envelope is enclosed for this purpose.

Yours sincerely

K R Merrett
Secretary

*A very proud moment. Realising my dream of becoming a professional footballer at the biggest club
in the world.*

Playing at The Cliff against my old Bolton Lads Club team-mate Neil Hart.

The Exeter City squad photo 1992/93 season. A lifeline thrown and opportunity for a new start.

They say the true mark of a player is whether he can do it on a cold, wet, windy and muddy night in Stoke. Here's proof I could!

The sheer joy and jubilation of scoring my first league goal against Stockport County at St James's Park.

Receiving my 1992/93 young player of the year award from Exeter City chairman Cliff Hill.

Captured in action during an away game for Exeter. Whoever designed that kit has a lot to answer for!

I really enjoy my commentary work with BBC Radio Devon. Here I am meeting Alan McInally before an away fixture at Sheffield Wednesday.

Professional Footballers Association
2 Oxford Court, Bishopsgate, Manchester M2 3WQ
Telephone: 0161-236 0575   Fax: 0161-228 7229

Chief Executive: Gordon Taylor M.A., B.Sc. (Econ.)

MM/KJM

eptember 1995

E Barrett
sor Insurance Brokers Ltd
House
166 Borough High Street
on SE1 IJR

Bob

Alan Tonge

writing with regard to the above former contract player at Exeter City F.C who
ained a serious injury to his back in October 1993 which resulted in surgery in
1994. Despite intensive rehabilitation he has been advised by the specialist to
prematurely from full time professional football and I enclose a medical report
h confirms this.

uld be pleased for you to process a claim on the player's behalf for his benefits
r the Football League Accident Insurance scheme.

s sincerely

J McGuire
stant Chief Executive

Probably the saddest letter I've ever received. Written confirmation that my professional football career was over.

With my beautiful daughter Lauren and son Sam. I'm incredibly proud of both of them.

About to receive my doctorate during my PhD graduation at Liverpool Cathedral. A very proud moment indeed.

Chapter 13

I'm Not Really Here

THE LAST few weeks of my time at United as my contract ran down were a bit of a blur. Probably because I was just going through the motions and still dealing with the heartbreak of being moved on, knowing my future looked very uncertain.

With it being the end of the season, training sessions weren't really structured and I remember playing a lot of five-a-sides at The Cliff, where Nobby Stiles took us because Eric Harrison was having some problems with his health. It all felt a bit strange, like I was just clocking in and out, waiting for it to be over so I could try to move on with my life. It was hard to turn up every day with that in the back of your mind and I'm sure the other lads who found themselves in the same situation felt it too.

We still had our end-of-season fixtures to complete, which started with the Blue Stars tournament over in Switzerland. It was a competition synonymous with United, who had been sending teams there since the days of the Busby Babes and always stayed at the same hotel. The club took a decent party that year, which included Nobby, Kiddo, Les Olive, Bobby Charlton and Sir Matt Busby.

Although he was getting on a bit by that stage, Sir Matt was a familiar face to us all from around the club and would occasionally appear to watch our matches. On the first evening, a group of us were sitting in the foyer of the hotel chatting and playing cards when he came wandering over. I remember him saying in his gravelly Scottish accent, 'Alright boys?'

The hairs on your arm stood up and we were a bit scared of him because this was a massive figure in the history of Manchester United. I think I managed to mumble, 'Yeah, all good thank you, Sir Matt.'

'As long as you're enjoying yourselves, that's the main thing.'

That line has always stuck with me because that's how his teams played isn't it – by enjoying themselves and making people happy. He ambled off, leaving us all a little bit awestruck.

The tournament itself was a strange one and I remember Adrian Doherty being on that trip, making an ill-fated comeback from the knee injury he'd suffered a few months earlier. There's a photo of us all where Oliver Kay picked up that he's standing quite gingerly.

I played in every match but was dropped for the final, which I was very annoyed about. It was another slap in the face after being played on the left wing against Sheffield United for the reserves. This time I didn't even make the bench; they were probably looking at the future and it was pretty obvious that I was now surplus to requirements. Part of me didn't want the lads to win the final, which may seem selfish or petty, but I just didn't feel involved anymore.

That trip did end on a more positive note, however, when, rather bizarrely, it presented the opportunity for us to play alongside Sir Bobby Charlton. The Brazilian team Botafogo were over there and asked United to play a friendly after the competition itself had finished, with the special request that Sir Bobby turned out for us. The whole thing was a very surreal experience. I'd been brought up on my dad telling me stories of the 'Holy Trinity' of Best, Law and Charlton, and now here I was playing alongside the latter in a match for Manchester United! He was in his early 50s by that point but absolutely ran the show and scored as well. He was unbelievable and you could only imagine how good he must have been in his prime. He was pinging balls all over the pitch, dropping his shoulder and knocking it out wide, just schooling everybody. He could manipulate the ball on either foot and still had his absolute piledriver of a shot. We won 3-0 and it's a special memory to have shared a pitch with arguably one of the greatest players the game has ever produced.

There were still a few more memories to be made. The first team had reached the final of the European Cup Winners' Cup so the club took all the reserves, youth players and staff over to the match against Barcelona in Rotterdam.

That was another interesting episode and not for all the right reasons. A lot of us on that trip knew we were being released by that point, which probably partly explains what unfolded. It got very boozy and I think some of the lads were trying to drown their sorrows. Honestly, it was like a stag do. The whole thing was done as a round trip, so we didn't stay over. The plan was that we'd fly out and get there for late morning, do a bit of sightseeing (drinking) during the day, watch the final in the evening and then get on the coach back to the airport straight after it finished.

We got to Amsterdam before midday as planned and ended up on this boat trip along the river. Bottles of Amstel started being passed through the group and we were on it there for a couple of hours before visiting a few bars, mixing with the United fans. We were in our club blazers, joining in with the singing, and they treated us like heroes.

I had a few but wasn't really a big drinker at that stage of my life; however, some of the other lads were absolutely bladdered. We then had to get a coach from Amsterdam to Rotterdam, which is where things really started to get messy. There were lads being sick and pissing in carrier bags because there was no toilet on the coach. I think Ralph Milne threw a can of beer at a youth-team player called Alan McReavie, which then led to a scuffle and one of them ending up with a cut eye.

I don't know whether the coach driver complained because we got pulled over by the police and all had to line up next to the coach by the side of the road. When we finally got to the ground a few of the lads didn't make it inside to watch the match and instead stayed on the coach to sleep off the booze. I know a few of them were called into Fergie's office when we got back and told they were a disgrace to the club. He was absolutely fuming about it.

The atmosphere and the final itself was brilliant, though. I was next to Kieran Toal, and the whole ground was singing 'Sit Down' by James, which was popular at the time. I remember all the flags, colours and the enormity of the crowd being pretty striking. I think a lot of United fans still talk about Rotterdam as one of their favourite European aways, and it was a great thing to be part of.

Ronald Koeman scored a free kick for Barça and I think Clayton Blackmore cleared one off the line late on, but two goals from Mark Hughes sealed it for us to pick up the trophy, which was incredible to witness, although bittersweet in a way. The club was turning a corner and things were looking up at last, which as a fan I was buzzing about, but I knew joining in with the celebrations that I wasn't going to be part of the future.

All that was left was a trip to Trinidad, which was an interesting place to visit. We were warned not to venture too far from the hotel, and despite there being plenty of wealth evident, there was lots of poverty too. It was run down in places, with loads of corrugated iron living accommodation. We played two matches, one against their national team's under-19s, which included a young Dwight Yorke, who was ridiculously good. I think we lost 3-1. The conditions were terrible and they were more used to it than us. Not to mention being a decent team who gave us the runaround.

The heat was incredible; it was absolutely sweltering and I had pools of sweat dripping off my arms. The pitch was just baked grass and I probably lost about half a stone before being brought off at half-time with a collarbone injury after colliding with a post. I remember as we got on the coach afterwards that loads of their fans started shouting and banging on the windows. Nobby Stiles had come on the tour with us and told the driver to stop the bus. He got off and, as he walked towards them, they ran off. It was classic Nobby, brave as a lion.

It was my last hurrah in a Manchester United shirt but I'd mentally checked out by that point anyway. Dwight Yorke may have been part of United's future but I knew I wasn't going to be and just wanted to focus on what I was going to do next. Those last few weeks were like being in a relationship break-up where you're still living with your partner while you get things sorted. There wasn't much stuff to collect from The Cliff at the end. I maybe went in to get my boots and shin pads but you literally just leave out the back door and they move on without you.

And then in the days that follow it starts to dawn on you – it's all over …

The Second Half

Chapter 14

Never Give Up

I SLUNG my bag across the living room and slumped down on the sofa. 'Where do I go from here?' The summer of 1991 was a tough one as I pondered my next steps after being cut loose by United.

The manager and Eric Harrison had said they'd try to fix me up with a new club and there was talk of interest from Nottingham Forest and Leicester City but it didn't come to anything. I remember chasing the gaffer to see whether anyone had enquired about me but he was in America for about six weeks that summer so I couldn't get hold of him.

His assistant Archie Knox did give me some sage advice when I bumped into him on the forecourt at Old Trafford during my final weeks with the club. Archie was also moving on, joining up with Walter Smith at Rangers. I must have looked forlorn and almost melancholic but he gave me some words of encouragement. He told me to keep going, never give up and keep looking for opportunities. It was appreciated.

My dad wasn't very happy with the way I was treated by United and felt I hadn't been looked after by the club. Fergie ended up ringing our house and they had a conversation. He then sent a letter saying I was a credit to Manchester United, that I'd never given him a moment's trouble and had always given my all for the club both physically and mentally. It was a nice gesture but scant consolation. At the age of 19 you're not fully mature so I felt very let down and disappointed. I'd been cut adrift on memory bliss.

Only the very top players had agents back then so I desperately phoned round clubs to ask for a trial and ended up doing pre-season with my local club Bolton Wanderers after their manager Phil Neal agreed to have a look at me. I was there for two or three weeks and remember training with the likes of Phil Brown, Sammy Lee, Mark Seagraves and Julian Darby when they mixed the reserves and the first team. I also featured in a couple of friendlies against non-league teams, one of which was against Lancaster City.

Nothing came of it; Bolton's reserve-team manager broke the news to me that they wouldn't be taking things further. They said they didn't think I was any better than the players they already had in my position. It was another blow and I was sinking lower and lower. My motivation and fight was running near empty. There can be a lot of grudges held in football and maybe they remembered that I'd chosen United over them as a schoolboy. At the time I probably should have looked at other clubs to see what they could offer and might have got more opportunities to progress there, but ultimately I'd let my heart rule my head because I was from a family full of United fans and it was an opportunity to live my dream. Hindsight is a wonderful thing.

I still felt I had something to offer in the game and just wanted someone to give me an opportunity, so I went to play non-league football for a bit with Horwich RMI. I enjoyed it but knew it could only be temporary if I was to harbour any ambitions of resurrecting my career. It was more to maintain fitness while I weighed up my options. We trained twice a week with a match on a Saturday afternoon, and I played a handful of times for them in the three months or so that I was there.

The matches were fast-paced and physical. It was rough and ready on pitches that weren't the best and you were playing alongside lads where most of them had a proper day job. It was a different world. The manager Ken Wright was quite big in non-league circles and there were a few other lads in the team who had just been released by Football League clubs, so I guess we had some common ground.

It was a shock to the system, having been at United only a few months before and playing alongside Sir Bobby Charlton to now be turning out against the likes of Emley and Gainsborough Trinity. I remember seeing George Knight, the scout who had got me to United at one of the matches I played for Horwich, and wondering what he must have been thinking.

Things were looking bleak but football is full of surprises, and before my thoughts started to turn towards getting a day job alongside playing part-time, it threw me a lifeline. In life you have to fight for almost everything but sometimes things happen by chance and appear from nowhere.

Alan Ball was from my local area, Farnworth in Bolton, which is next to Little Lever. One of my mum and dad's neighbours phoned him about my predicament as he'd just taken the manager's job down at Exeter City. He remembered me from the Moscow trip a couple of years earlier and I believe he'd also watched me play for United reserves so he rang our house and invited me down for a trial. As a 19-year-old I had absolutely no idea where Exeter was. My dad had to draw me a map because there were no satnavs back then, so I embarked upon a new adventure in my little Ford Fiesta. My family were very upset as I drove away and I guess it was a bit like some youngsters when they go off to university, living away from home for the first time.

Looking back, it took a lot of courage because it was a long way and involved navigating several motorways to reach the south coast. The furthest I'd driven in a car prior to that was probably Blackpool! It took me about five hours and I remember 'Wind of Change' by The Scorpions blaring out on my cassette player. It felt like destiny.

They told me to go to the Near Post, which was the name of the club shop. I went in and told them who I was and that I was there for a trial. They gave me some directions to the digs where I'd be staying, which was a big house owned by a couple called Roz and Geoff Colling. I was there with five or six other players, including Graham Waters, Kev Miller, Dave Cooper, Tony Frankland and John Hodge. They were all good players and, most importantly, good lads who were trying to make their way in the game.

I ended up sharing a room with John Hodge, who I knew from when he'd been on trial at United previously. It was like being in a whirlwind where you were completely outside your comfort zone and didn't know what was coming next. It was uncomfortable but it was an opportunity to get my career going again at a Football League club who were in the equivalent of League One at the time. The alternative was to get a job in the real world, which I didn't feel ready for yet. I had the fire to believe I wasn't finished but, make no mistake, this was probably last chance saloon.

I was there for a couple of weeks initially and the trial went well. I threw everything into it because I was fighting for my football career, not really wanting to return to Little Lever having failed again.

The former Southampton, Arsenal and England midfielder Steve Williams was the reserve-team manager alongside his role as a senior pro in the first team. I remember we played a practice match against Torquay United on Exeter's Cat and Fiddle training ground and Justin Fashanu turned out for them. I'd come up against him before while playing for United's reserves during his brief spell at Manchester City. He was a very physical player like his brother John and had left Tony Gill with the worst black eye I've ever seen.

My hard work paid off when they offered me a contract until the end of the season, which was only about six months or so. It didn't give me a lot of security but was better than nothing. It was something to build on and I remember Alan Ball saying to me, 'You've been a lucky lad, son. It's up to you now.'

Bally had been released by Bolton Wanderers at 16 for being too small and ended up a World Cup winner at 21. I think he could probably empathise with my struggle and wanted to give this young lad who had travelled to the other end of the country a chance.

It was a breakthrough for my career but wasn't without sacrifice. Me upping sticks and moving to the south coast sadly spelled the beginning of the end of my relationship with my first girlfriend, which was really hard because we'd been together since we were 14. They say the first cut is the deepest and I'd fully agree with that. The challenges of training or playing miles away plus the lack of security with my contract situation and relatively low wages meant it wasn't really viable for her to move down there with me, unfortunately. She was very close to her family so circumstances drove us apart eventually. It's another example of professional football being a cruel mistress and what it puts you through.

I started out in Exeter's reserve team, which was a decent standard where we usually played against non-league teams. There were quite a few younger lads so I was more of a senior player, which was beneficial for my development and pushed me on a bit. Things continued to move in the right direction when a bit of luck and a few injuries meant I got the call to finally make my professional debut on 8 February 1992, just shy of my 20th birthday, in a home match against Wigan Athletic.

It felt great to turn up at the club's ground St James Park on matchday in my suit, and it was what I'd been waiting for. I was nervous and early on you're just looking to get a feel for the standard but I'd played against decent players before. I had a good game and we were probably unlucky not to get anything from it, losing 1-0 to a late winner.

Playing alongside me for Exeter that day was a lad called Ian Thompstone, who was a year older but from the same area of Bolton. We'd even attended the same secondary school and sort of grown up together with the tag of being the best young prospects in the area. Ian had been signed by Manchester City, where he scored in his only first-team appearance for the club before being moved on. Now here we were playing in the same team a good 250 miles from where we grew up. It's strange how things work out sometimes. Unfortunately, Ian was moved on very harshly indeed not too long after. We played Bury at Gigg Lane towards the end of the season and put in a poor performance, losing 3-1. I was brought on as a late sub but by that stage Bally had gone down the tunnel to sit in the bath because he'd seen enough. We were in the dressing room afterwards, when he walked in and told Ian that he was going to Halifax and that the deal was all sorted. I felt so sorry for Ian because he'd only just finished furnishing his apartment in Exeter and his girlfriend had moved down too. It was absolutely brutal and shows that as players back then we were just very weak pawns in someone else's game.

I stayed in the team for a 5-1 defeat at Chester City a few days after the Wigan match, where I came up against Arthur Albiston, who was playing left-back for them, which was quite surreal. Two defeats in the space of a week maybe wasn't the best of starts but I felt I'd done okay and it was a foot on the ladder. I dropped back down to the reserves after that as a few of the regular first-team players started to return. I was a little disappointed not to be involved in an impressive win at Bolton a couple of weeks later, which obviously would have held some sentimental value.

Things looked promising though, and at the end of 1991/92 they offered me a year's contract. I'd managed to carve myself an opportunity and if my time at United had given me anything it was instilling that fight which meant it wasn't in my nature to give up. The fire had been flickering but it hadn't gone out, and with the right desire in football and in life things can happen for you.

That year of my life was a turbulent one but when I look back now the thing I'm most proud of is that after the heartbreak of being released by United, with my confidence on the floor, I found the courage to get back up again. A lot don't, and drift out of professional football.

Chapter 15

Win or Lose, We're On the Booze

THE 1992/93 season didn't get off to the best of starts for me or my former employers Manchester United who lost their opening two league matches, but fortunately for us both it wasn't a sign of things to come.

It was my first pre-season where I had a sniff of being involved with a first team so I was keen to impress, but after a couple of days I wasn't feeling so clever. I thought I was just fatigued from all the running and that I could push through it, but I ended up collapsing at the end of a six-mile run down Exmouth beach. I was in a bad way and the physio said my pulse rate was ridiculous. It was like being hit with a sledgehammer. Of course, the other lads thought it was hilarious and gave me the nickname 'Lazarus' because I'd seemingly come back from the dead. I was given a bottle of Lucozade to aid my recovery, which they charged me for when we got back to the training ground! It turned out that I had glandular fever, which kept me out for the first couple of months.

Having a full pre-season behind you can make a massive difference but after a while I began to battle my way into contention, making the starting XI for a match at Huddersfield, which we drew 0-0 at their old ground Leeds Road, albeit in slightly strange circumstances. I was initially named on the bench but Ronnie Jepson had got stuck in traffic so I took his place in central midfield until he finally made it to the ground and replaced me at half-time. I partnered Steve Williams in the middle of the park and remember him talking to me a lot throughout that first half because I was still quite raw. I'd found out before kick-off that Eric Harrison was in the crowd, which maybe unsettled me a bit, but I managed to hold my own until Jeppo had negotiated his traffic jam.

I played at right-back in a memorable 3-2 win over Reading. I was behind Scott Hiley, who scored the perfect hat-trick in a brilliant game of football. They had Shaka Hislop in goal and Jimmy Quinn playing up front, who got sent off early on, which was a big boost for us. Coming back from that match we all met up in a pub and I remember glowing inside after hearing Bally say after a few pints what a good player Alan Tonge was! He also offered me a two-year contract on that trip. We were playing snooker in the lounge of the hotel and he asked if he could have a word. I was absolutely buzzing when he told me, because it would finally give me some proper stability and mean I could concentrate on my football.

The week before Christmas I came off the bench for the last 20 minutes of a 2-2 home draw with Burnley. What was funny about that match, though, was I remember warming up down the touchline in front of the away fans, and among the expected banter I heard one of them shout, 'Alan?' Bewildered, I turned around by the corner flag, having no idea who it was. 'I work with your dad at British Gas!' I was about 250 miles away from home but it's a small world. I think we had a little chat before I realised Bally was waving at me from the dugout to get stripped and get on. My dad's colleague did wish me all the best if I recall correctly, which was nice of him.

I had a couple of days off after the match so decided to head back up north to see the family before the busy Christmas schedule and got caught speeding on my way home. You could say I managed to get four points that day, one for the draw against Burnley and another three with the speeding ticket!

After that all eyes were on our Boxing Day clash with Plymouth Argyle in the Devon derby, but I thought I'd blown any chance I had of being involved following a poor performance in the reserves away at Cardiff in midweek. The gaffer came to watch and hammered me afterwards. I was gutted but maybe he was using a few mind games to get a bit more out of me because I was still picked for the big match and it must have stirred something.

The lead-up was brilliant. It was an early kick-off, 11am, because of the situation with the policing. It's a fiercely contested derby and Exeter had got themselves into a spot of bother with the Football League that season during the build-up to Christmas for their choice of half-time entertainment, involving a man dressed in a seven-foot turkey costume complete with Argyle shirt being chased across the pitch and 'shot'. The powers that be didn't see the funny side so the act was stopped as it was felt it could incite trouble between the fans and was indeed not in the best of taste.

Plymouth were a good team, with Peter Shilton in goal, who was also their manager at the time. It felt crazy that just a couple of years previously I'd watched him play for England at Italia 90 on the TV and now I was lining up against him. I've heard since that the Exeter fans were taunting him during the match, singing that Bally had won the World Cup.

They had a guy called Steve Castle in midfield who was their captain and a solid player. Paul Dalton played on the wing, who had been at United with me a few years earlier, but my instructions that day were to mark Warren Joyce and follow him everywhere because he was their playmaker who made them tick. Bally was a big admirer and I think he tried to sign him a few times. A lot of their play went through Joyce and we knew that if we took him out of the equation we had a better chance of winning. You don't seem to see man-marking employed as much in modern football but if it's done right it can be very effective.

It was just one of those days where everything went really well and I had a great game, getting plenty of tackles in. I set up our first goal, a Peter Whiston header from a nice cross into the box after about quarter of an hour, which given the kick-off time must be in with a shout of being the earliest goal in the day scored in Football League history. We won 2-0 but had three goals disallowed, so we battered them, and to cap it all off I got man of the match, which I was absolutely buzzing about. It was a massive day for the club and I still get nice messages from Exeter fans talking about that match. If I could live another day in my life from start to finish that would be it because it's the happiest memory I have in football. We beat them away 3-0 later in the season too, a match I wasn't involved in but it was nice to be part of a team that had given the fans a double over our local rivals.

The highs kept coming, and looking back it was probably my best spell of football. I picked up another man of the match award away at Stoke City. They say the mark of a player is whether he can do it on a cold, wet and windy night in Stoke, and I could. I've still got the newspaper clipping to prove it!

There was a lot of hostility towards us over the way that Bally had left them prior to joining Exeter and I think their fans threw boiling hot tea over him in the reverse fixture at St James Park. He got us really wound up beforehand in the dressing room and

I remember him saying to us, 'They'll all be dragging themselves out of their armchairs tonight to watch the massacre. Go and prove them all wrong.'

Lou Macari was Stoke's manager at the time and he had a kitman called Neil Baldwin, or 'Nello' as he was affectionately known. Nello was adorned in a chicken fancy dress outfit that night and kept knocking on our dressing room door and wandering in. I think he was just trying to wind Bally up.

I was given another marking job on a lad called Kevin Russell, with instructions to follow him everywhere and get my digs in when I could. We went 1-0 up through Andy Cook before they equalised and then Scott Daniels was sent off for a foul as the last man, but it was a decent point away from home considering they were going for promotion, while we were struggling a bit down the bottom of the table. Funnily enough, I believe that fixture in January 1993 is the last time the two teams crossed paths at the time of writing, as they were promoted that season.

We had some great results, beating Wigan Athletic at Springfield Park and getting to the southern area final of the Autoglass Trophy. I played in most of those matches, which included victories over Swansea and Brighton, before Port Vale beat us over two legs in the final. I had the thrill of scoring my first professional goal on that run, against Reading. Scott Hiley crossed from the right, Eamonn Dolan nodded it back and I just neatly took the chance from about 12 yards on the half-volley.

I found the back of the net again a few days later against Stockport County from the edge of the box. I took a swing at it and honestly thought the keeper was going to save it but he kind of palmed it into the top of the net. Two in two – prolific! The emotion of scoring is unbelievable. That exhilaration you feel when you see the ball hit the back of the net, the crowd going mental and you're punching the air. It's the best feeling and difficult to replicate when you've finished playing. My dad still says that one of the proudest moments of his life was seeing that 'Tonge' had scored for Exeter while trying to follow the Stockport match back home on Teletext. There were no live updates in those days and my mum used to phone Club Call. For those who might not remember, Club Call was a service that gave regular updates on a particular match while charging a premium rate for the call. My mum says the phone bill used to be through the roof!

I had a steady relationship with Bally and I think he liked me. My fitness and attitude were good, I trained well and always gave 100 per cent, which I think the fans appreciated too. Coming from a club as big as United, there's usually increased expectations on you, which I was conscious of, but it gave me confidence that someone as respected as a World Cup winner was giving me the opportunity to play first-team football. We had a connection and I think he understood me. I remember him saying: 'You just do enough to win a race.'

It was interesting and maybe mentally I was still recovering from the trauma of being released by United. When you've had a negative experience you sometimes naturally go into yourself but I think he could see that I had more in my locker than I was perhaps showing. When I arrived at Exeter I was probably quite introverted in the way I played the game because all the confidence and expression had been hammered out of me.

I found out recently that I was booked in seven of my first ten appearances for the club so I was maybe a bit overzealous and eager to please, having come from an environment where big tackles were encouraged. Referees in those days were generally more lenient but we did pick up a lot of bookings as a squad and eventually the FA began to ask questions. I remember an article in the local newspaper where Bally said that we were a young team just finding our way.

He was small in stature but a giant of a person, similar to Fergie in that he could lose his temper and they were both winners. He'd been a great footballer and demanded that from his players but it's fair to say we weren't on his level so he was often very red in the face at half-time. I remember being an unused substitute for one match where we hadn't got a result and he was fuming. We came into the dressing room and he went round everyone giving them a bollocking. I thought I'd be exempt from it as I hadn't featured, but when he got to me he carried on his tirade and bellowed, 'And you Tongey, that's the worst fucking warm-up I've ever seen in my life!'

He'd often stop training sessions if he was disappointed with the standard or felt that the level needed raising and would join in with the five-a-sides on a Friday morning. He was in his late 40s by that point but still one step ahead of everyone else, flicking the ball round corners first time, and it was difficult to get near him. It was a bit like training with the first team at United, where you'd come away from it thinking you needed to work harder and get better. He must have been absolutely electric in his prime.

Bally had a lot of contacts in the game and brought the former Rangers manager Jock Wallace with us on a pre-season trip to Cornwall. He was daft as a brush and a bit sergeant major-like. He loved his horse racing and could normally be found down at Exeter races or Newton Abbot. He was pals with Mick Channon who had just started training racehorses at the time, so he'd often come in with a few tips for us to get on down the bookies. There was even talk at one stage of us all buying shares in a racehorse and keeping it at the training ground, with its own stables being built. Sadly the idea never got off the ground, which was a shame because it could have saved the groundsman a job cutting the grass!

Bally liked a drink and would often socialise with us, telling stories about his England days and how he thought of himself as a little ginger kid from Bolton lining up against some of the greatest players there's ever been, like Pelé and Jairzinho. He was good pals with Bobby Moore, who sadly passed away while I was at Exeter. I remember Bally being upset about it. He was also best mates with Nobby Stiles as they'd come from similar upbringings, and I believe after the World Cup Final in 1966 he'd swapped shirts with Nobby rather than one of the German players.

After a few drinks he had a habit of knocking on players' hotel rooms for a chat in the early hours of the morning. You'd often try to ignore it because if he did come in it was difficult to get rid of him and he'd just spend ages talking and telling us how great we were. He loved his players and was very big on team spirit. One of his strengths was that he knew how to keep a group together, which I think he'd learned from the likes of Sir Alf Ramsey during his playing career and taken it with him into management. One of his favourite phrases was: 'Generals can't win wars on their own, nor can foot soldiers but together they might.'

He had time for different players and understood their characters. He knew that you needed leaders in a team and your technical players but also lads who could scrap and put a shift in. I'd predominantly been a right-back or centre-half at United but I think he saw I could play a bit, so he often picked me to do a job in midfield. He took the time to recognise players' strengths and how to apply them in matches, because he used to give me a lot of marking jobs. 'Just stick with him today but go and play when you can.'

I loved playing for him because he gave me the freedom to play and I felt valued as a member of his squad. I remember him turning down an approach from Torquay United, who were interested in signing me at one point. I also got a nice mention in his autobiography as part of a group of players he brought to Exeter City who all did well for the club, which was lovely. The man was a legend.

I could feel a bit of self-esteem coming back and was pretty content living in a beautiful part of the country. It was much more laid-back down there as opposed to the rush of the city that I was used to but it allowed me to grow as a footballer and as a person. At United all your kit would be laid out for you and you could have new boots whenever you wanted them. At Exeter the facilities were more basic. You had to wash all your own kit so would often find yourself in the launderette for a couple of hours waiting for it to finish.

The club was going through some financial struggles so there were a couple of occasions when wages weren't paid on time. At one point the comedian Freddie Starr tried to buy the club and turned up to training once, probably just to spread a bit of humour. He told us that whoever scored in our next match had to do a certain celebration for the crowd. It was good fun but his takeover didn't go through, sadly.

There was no canteen at the training ground so we'd usually just get a sandwich on our way back to the digs and then all sit round the table for tea in the evenings. In our downtime we'd chat, have a bit of banter and sometimes go to the local driving range at Fingle Glen. You were in that professional footballer's routine of training and resting between fixtures on a Saturday and often midweek too.

I shared a room in digs with Dave Cooper, another young pro who had been at Luton Town as an apprentice before winding up at Exeter. He was a decent left-back who the fans christened 'Mad Dog'. Coops was a great lad and my best mate down there. We became very close and had a great social life together. We always looked out for each other and I can remember pulling him away from bother on nights out. He wouldn't take any messing and didn't suffer any fools. He played several times for Exeter City but suffered a shocking leg break from a 50/50 tackle, meaning he had to have a rod inserted down his shin, which sadly finished his career. He's a coach at Crystal Palace now and I'm still in touch with him. He always talks about throwing rolled-up socks at me in my sleep to stop me snoring. He still says I'm the loudest snorer he ever heard and that the drawers on the dressing table used to go in and out!

I remember the owner of the digs had a pellet rifle, which Coops clocked and asked whether he could have a go. I had a red Ford Orion with a retractable sunroof and when it went dark he'd get me to open it so he could stand on the passenger seat with the rifle, while I drove with my lights off across the field at the bottom of the road. On his command I'd turn the lights on and he'd fire at rabbits that would be scarpering everywhere, like Exeter City's very own version of Elmer Fudd! What a character he was. A brilliantly funny lad and I loved him to bits.

I was also close to Danny Bailey and we've remained in contact over the years. Dan was a rock-solid midfielder and like Coops you'd want him alongside you in the trenches because he was a warrior. He looked after himself and was teetotal with a good physique. A top lad. He had this red sports car and I remember an away fixture at Bournemouth where I travelled but wasn't in the squad. He must have been staying over after the match because he asked me to drive it there for him. I had to follow the team coach in it and remember jumping red lights and all sorts to keep up so I didn't get lost. I met Harry Redknapp that day, too. He was chirpy and big pals with Bally. I seem to remember us winning 3-1 with Eamonn Dolan scoring one of the goals and pulling his shirt over his head to celebrate with the fans.

It was a very friendly club and Bally had used his connections to assemble a decent squad, with some top pros who had good pedigree or lads who went on to bigger things. Kevin Miller was a high-quality keeper who later played in the Premier League, Steve Williams had won a handful of England caps under Bobby Robson, Martin Phillips was a tricky winger who got a big move to Manchester City, Stevie Moran had been a talented player who partnered Kevin Keegan up front for Southampton, Scott Hiley was a classy right-back who got a good move to Birmingham City and Stuart Storer also had memorable spells at Bolton Wanderers and Brighton & Hove Albion.

There were also plenty of very good pros with varying degrees of experience, such as Jon Brown, Andy Harris, Eamonn Collins, Andy Cook, Ronnie Jepson, Vince Hilaire, Eamonn Dolan, Kevin Bond, Toby Redwood, Scott Daniels, Peter Whiston, Russell Coughlin, John Hodge, Mark Robson and Craig Taylor.

It was a great group of lads and there were plenty of 'team-bonding' sessions on a Saturday night over a few beers, which I grew into as a way of winding down. The drinking culture in English football was still widespread so most of the lads would partake and it didn't feel like you were doing anything wrong. You'd just make sure you trained doubly hard on a Monday to sweat out that weekend's excess and we'd never drink less than 48 hours before a match. That was the rule.

Things were starting to change in England with the arrival of players like Eric Cantona but it takes time to filter down through the pyramid. Nowadays clubs employ dietary experts and nutritionists, therefore they understand the full importance of recovery between matches and that sinking ten pints and having a Chinese takeaway on a weekend probably isn't the best idea.

We had some great times together though, and you never forget those bonds with former team-mates. The culture was a bit mental and we had some serious drinkers there. Russell Coughlin was absolutely mad and Ronnie Jepson never seemed to feel the effects of alcohol. We used to go to a pub called the Valiant Soldier on a Saturday night, where it wouldn't be uncommon for Coops to do the yard of ale. He'd sometimes crack raw eggs in the bottom of it too. Madness.

I remember going to a nightclub that had all the girls from the *Sunday Sport* there. We had our pictures taken and I'm not sure where those ended up.

The annual Christmas party was always epic and would take place when we didn't have a match for a few days, to allow time for recovery. I remember we did fancy dress one year. Coops and I were dressed up as the Scousers from *Harry Enfield*, with black permed wigs and moustaches. One of the lads was a Viking, another was Scooby Doo, we had a pantomime horse and I'm sure we had the Pink Panther there too. We went out dressed in our outfits and it turned into a mad one. We were all plastered and ended up in a nightclub where it all kicked off with another group. On the periphery, it must have been quite a sight to see various characters throwing punches and grappling with each other. A surreal moment. I honestly couldn't believe what was going on.

We all went paintballing once, which is usually a sign that things aren't going well on the pitch and clubs try to think outside of the box for ways to boost morale. It was hilarious. I remember watching Coops fit a silencer to his paint gun as we were getting ready. A reporter from the local paper, the *Express and Echo*, came down to take a picture but when he pointed the camera at us Coops shot the poor guy in the bollocks from close range! It must have been very painful but we were all in hysterics.

I was young and enjoying life. I'd never really felt part of it at United but I think coming to Exeter from a big club meant I was accepted and fortunate that many of the people down there seemed to take to me, particularly Sam Partington and Tony Agger, who I met in the Barley Mow pub and became great friends with. They really looked out for me and Sam was the best man at my wedding.

The 90s was a great time to be young, and back home Manchester was exploding with the likes of Stone Roses and Oasis, so maybe they thought I brought some of that with me. I made lots of mates down there, although looking back some of them weren't really for the right reasons as I was probably spending more time drinking than I should have been doing.

A group of us went back in 2021 to play a vets match and I remember driving round with Coops visiting all our old haunts, which mainly consisted of the digs, pubs and bookies! A lot of it's just blurred in a drunken haze because when we weren't playing football it was like an ongoing stag do. I was actually sponsored by the Barley Mow in the club's matchday programme, which says it all really.

Booze unfortunately played a larger part in my run-in towards the end of the season than it should have done. I returned to my hometown when we played Bolton Wanderers at Burnden Park in

March. It was an opportunity to maybe prove a point to them for not signing me but it was just too much on the day as we lost 4-1 and I did feel that I'd let myself down a bit. Feeling the pressure coming home and having all my friends and family come to watch, it was hard to face them all afterwards.

After that I wasn't really involved in the first team for the final few weeks as the season drew to a close with us battling to keep our heads above the water and avoid relegation. In the penultimate fixture, against Port Vale, we were winning 1-0, which would have been enough to secure survival, but the referee awarded them a dubious late penalty that they equalised from and all hell broke loose. There was a massive pitch invasion on the final whistle and somebody punched the referee! There's still footage of it on YouTube and it's not pleasant viewing.

Tensions were running very high as that set up a final match at Fulham where we needed to get something but as I'd not featured for a while I thought my season was over and I'd just be sitting in the stands at Craven Cottage supporting the lads.

The Thursday before was quite a warm day. It had been a tough season and we'd been under a lot of pressure throughout, so me and Coops decided to have a few drinks as he was injured anyway. We bought a couple of crates of beer from the off-licence near our digs and sat in the garden in the sun working our way through them. The empty Budweiser bottles became piled high in a pyramid on the lawn. It turned into a heavy session and I think we might have even gone for a few more in town afterwards.

I felt really rough for training on the Friday morning but wasn't too concerned. I thought I'd just be going through the motions while the lads who were involved on Saturday finalised their preparations and set pieces for the big match the next day. We had a team meeting in the gym where Bally did a lot of his pre-match talks. I remember him coming in and going through the starting line-up: '... and Alan Tonge will come in at left-back'.

Oh shit! I was sitting at the back on a table and Coops was pissing himself laughing. It served me right for switching off, and now the need to prepare myself physically and mentally was paramount.

We went out and did a bit of training where I felt all over the place, before setting off for the big smoke for our relegation decider, which I was going to have to play semi-hungover. When you've had a heavy session it takes a few days for it to get out of your system and I was definitely more nervous than usual, knowing that my preparation had been less than ideal. It was the biggest match of the season for Exeter and as a player you're very aware of the consequences if it goes wrong. It's a catastrophic thing for a football club to be relegated, as people can lose their jobs, so looking back it was very unprofessional on my part and not something I'm proud of.

I still felt ropey during the warm-up. Craven Cottage was a nice ground to play at though, and I remember us coming out in the corner and there being a decent crowd. Once the match started I just tried to keep it simple. I was up against a lad called Julian Hails who was their player of the season but I managed to keep him quiet by getting tight, although I did feel quite leggy towards the end when they started to put us under a bit of pressure. We held firm though, and Stuart Storer scored our goal, cutting in from the left-hand side. I remember jumping on his back and celebrating in front of our fans.

Thankfully things went in our favour on the day. Bolton beat Preston 2-0 to send them down and we battled to a 1-1 draw to secure our place in the Second Division for another season, finishing 19th in the table.

Jimmy Hill told me in the players' lounge afterwards that I'd done really well, which was nice, and I got a lot of praise in the match reports too. No one knew I was still half-pissed! In hindsight I dodged a bullet because if things hadn't gone well and Exeter had been relegated then I'd be looking back at that match with a lot of guilt. All's well that ends well. The Scottish golfer Sam Torrance once said he'd had a few pints of Guinness before a tournament and missed shooting a 59 by one shot. My advice to any young player is never prepare like that.

I'd enjoyed a good season as a squad player at a Football League club and picked up the club's young player of the year award, which I was absolutely thrilled about. To cap it all off United had finally won a league title for the first time in 26 years, which was great to see. It was a happy time that I look back on with a lot of fondness and I was looking forward to building on my progress over the following campaign.

It didn't seem like a huge deal at the time but, due to financial constraints, the club had reneged on their offer of a two-year contract and I remember being called into Bally's office for a chat. 'I've spoken to the board Tongey, and it's been decided we're only going to give you one year. I want you to take a year and trust me.'

Trust in football is non-existent, and looking back it left me vulnerable. I regret not signing that two-year deal straight away because things can change very quickly in professional football, as I was about to find out.

Chapter 16

Finished

I'D BEEN feeling a bit of discomfort in my back for a while. I just wanted to keep playing but could feel it gradually getting worse and worse ...

The 1993/94 season was a lot more challenging than the previous campaign on many fronts. The club had signed a few players to increase competition for places and I arguably never got going. I found my first-team opportunities very limited and was used in the reserves a lot during the first half of the season as a more senior player to help the younger lads.

I did manage to make it through pre-season this time. We did a training camp with the Royal Marines at their nearby base in Lympstone, which was about a 20-minute drive away. A couple of our coaching staff were ex-marines and we'd sometimes go up there to use the facilities if our training pitches were flooded.

It was an interesting experience. We turned up, and going through the gates was like entering another world. We were all given khaki uniforms and they had us doing assault courses, climbing up ropes and dragging mats across the floor in their massive indoor sports hall where they set up different scenarios, such as a plane crash in the jungle. We all had different roles to play. You'd have to run across beams and piggyback your mate back to the start. It must have been part of their training and the fitness levels of their lads was ridiculous.

At the back of the camp there was a massive bay, which was basically a sea of mud, and they took us out there for a game of rugby. We were all caked in it, laying into each other with massive tackles, and they hosed us down afterwards. It was tough but something a bit different and good fun too.

We also played a friendly against Sheffield Wednesday, who boasted the likes of Chris Waddle, Des Walker, Carlton Palmer, David Hirst and Roland Nilsson in their ranks. It was a total mismatch and not ideal preparation at all for the new season; we were chasing shadows for 90 minutes and they turned us over 6-0. I bumped into Chris Waddle a few years ago while working for BBC Radio Manchester on a United match and he remembered it, funnily enough. He was a difficult player to play against and I think he nutmegged Coops and gestured to the crowd. Waddle was quality, a gangly runner who could beat a player two or three times if he needed to, and his technical ability was off the scale.

I made a return to Old Trafford early in the season, albeit not for footballing reasons. Coops and I managed to get tickets for the rematch of Chris Eubank vs Nigel Benn. I'd watched the first fight on ITV three years before, which was a real grudge match between two fighters at the top of their game and a cracking contest. I was quite a big boxing fan and had grown up watching the great Muhammad Ali fight on TV as he was coming towards the end of his career. Mike Tyson was in his prime when I was a teenager and knocking people out for fun for a few years before personal issues caught up with him and it all unravelled. I remember the plain black shorts and how he wouldn't wear a robe during his ring walk, like an old-school fighter. There was a huge buzz around him when he burst on the scene because he was something a bit different.

The 90s was a strong era for middleweights, with the likes of Michael Watson and Steve Collins also in the mix, so it felt like there was a good fight every couple of months or so. There was also Rob McCracken, who was up-and-coming at the time and knew Andy Harris, one of the lads at Exeter, so I remember watching a few of his fights. He challenged for a world title a few years later before going on to train both Carl Froch and Anthony Joshua.

That night at Old Trafford you could sense that more people in the crowd were rooting for Nigel Benn but personally I was a Eubank fan. I just loved his swagger and the fact that he was different. He was intelligent and eloquent, reciting poetry and philosophical quotations, not unlike my old United team-mate Aidy Doherty. The atmosphere was red-hot and I remember Coops commenting that the beer, which was a United version of Red Stripe, tasted like cat piss! The fight was billed as 'Judgement Day' and was another entertaining contest, which ended in a draw. It was a muted atmosphere afterwards as there was no winner, very subdued, and filing out I didn't know that I'd soon be fighting a battle of my own. One that I couldn't win.

The pain in my back was getting steadily worse and I started getting pins and needles down the side of my legs. Knowing my contract was up at the end of the season I thought I couldn't afford to take time out to get it looked at and carried on playing. In hindsight it was a stupid decision that did more harm than good.

I played one match for the first team against Swansea City at Vetch Field in the Autoglass Trophy around December 1993 and I was really struggling by that point. I remember smearing loads of Deep Heat on my lower back in the dressing room before we went out to play. I must have looked like the Ready Brek man! I shouldn't have played but we'd already gone through all the shape and tactics. I managed to complete the match but needed to see the physio the next day and that was the start of it all.

By that stage the pins and needles were constant and had spread to my hands and feet. Certain movements like bending down to pick something up were becoming more and more difficult. They sent me to Bristol for an MRI scan; Coops came with me and we went out for a few pints of Guinness the night before, which is probably an illustration of where I was mentally at the time.

I had the scan and the medical expert informed me they would need to operate. My discs had slipped and certain movements were causing them to touch on my spinal nerves. The surgeon said it was a real mess and that one bad bang or twist could have severed my spinal cord, leaving me paralysed and in a wheelchair, so it was extremely serious.

It was a time of great uncertainty; any footballer will tell you that being injured with no match to look forward to on a Saturday is miserable but I had the added stress of not knowing whether I'd get back from it. There was a big question mark over my future in the game and I was constantly worrying about whether I'd ever play again.

Things were changing at Exeter City too. Bally had gone to Southampton in January 1994 and I think my last first-team involvement was not long after under caretaker manager Peter Fox for a match against Bournemouth where I came on as a substitute for the last ten minutes. Terry Cooper, the former Leeds United player, was appointed as the new manager and I remember still trying to train in his early days at the club to prove myself, which was stupid looking back, considering what was at stake.

I could sense that Terry didn't really want me around. He wanted to bring his own players in, which was fair enough but it left me in the shit given my contract situation. I remember him telling me there were a couple of decent non-league clubs interested, which was hard because not only did it make it clear I was surplus to requirements, but it wasn't even a viable option as I couldn't train or play. I had a serious long-term injury that would require a period of rehabilitation and time if I was going to come back from it.

I knew I needed to concentrate on getting fit if I could but it was always at the back of my mind that come the end of June I'd effectively be unemployed so I was also plagued by worries of not being able to put food on the table. I know there were talks between the Professional Footballers' Association (PFA) and Exeter about extending my contract for another six months but nothing came of it. It was only later I realised that the club was in an extremely perilous financial position and simply couldn't afford to be paying someone who would basically be immobile for almost a year.

I had my first operation in April 1994 at Frenchay Hospital in Bristol, where four screws and two plates were inserted into the base of my spine. I was bedbound for ten days afterwards on a morphine drip, which was very frustrating as I was used to being so active. It was incredibly painful. I was really fed up and felt isolated, miles from home and a good two-hour journey from Exeter. I lay in my hospital bed watching the racing and the 1000 Guineas from Newmarket to try to pass the time. I also remember challenging myself to throw pips from the huge number of grapes I had into a light case above my bed. Anything to keep myself from going insane. While I was recovering, medics used to come round in the mornings with groups of students to analyse me as a case study.

'This is Alan, a professional footballer who has just had a spinal fusion.' I remember jokingly asking the doctor if he thought I'd be fit for Saturday, which triggered some laughter from the group. It's amazing really that I was still managing to find some humour at such a dark time.

I went through all the rehab, working with the club physio Mike Chapman, who was absolutely brilliant, but things had moved on, sadly, and I was becoming a forgotten man. After my contract expired in the summer Exeter allowed me to continue to use the facilities at the training ground but I was left to claim incapacity benefit to sustain some level of income.

Exeter City were relegated at the end of 1993/94 in the midst of some murky times, with the financial situation really beginning to bite. I'd been acutely aware of it throughout my time there as wages had been paid late on a few occasions but I didn't fully understand just how bad it was. The club nearly went bust the year after and I remember them producing a matchday programme with a black edge because there was a genuine fear it would be the last fixture the club would play. It's a difficult one because I still feel I could have got back from my injury with the right level of support but they weren't in a position to offer anything more as the future of the club itself was on the line.

It was a few months before I was even able to begin light training but when I did I was dealt another blow because I still had that tingling sensation, which meant more surgery. The decision on my future was made for me after I had the second operation in the autumn of 1994, when the surgeon delivered the news that I feared the most. They told me that my back would no longer stand up to the demands of professional football and recommended that I retire as I'd never be able to attain full fitness.

It was very final and I was absolutely devastated. Tears flowed. Football was everything to me. Imagine working your whole life in a career you love and then one day someone tells you that you can't do it anymore. It destroys you because that's what your whole identity is built around, and psychologically it's like a part of you dies.

At such a young age, I probably would have expected another decade of my career ahead of me but the thing with life is that you never know what's coming tomorrow and it had all gone pear-shaped after looking so promising. My retirement meant my potential as a footballer was never fully realised, which is quite sad to look back on. It's a small consolation to know I didn't throw it away but it leaves a question about how far I could have gone that I'll never be able to answer.

I received some help from the PFA in the form of insurance money, which totalled around £7,500, and Exeter's PFA representative Steve Wigley was magnificent in trying to fight my corner. It was a decent amount but money alone wasn't going to solve my problem. I'd be lying if I said I didn't spend some of it trying to drown my sorrows by going out drinking and walking into pubs flashing £50 notes, getting the drinks in for everyone. I couldn't be a footballer anymore but I was still trying to live like one while in the throes of my rehab with absolutely no idea what I was going to do next. The sense of purpose and meaning that I'd held for a long time had vanished and my daily routine and structure was gone. I still remember the day my P45 dropped through my letter box when my contract at Exeter expired, which was heartbreaking. There was no sentimentality and football moves on very quickly.

I was just cut adrift, which was disappointing, and I honestly wouldn't wish it on anyone. It was extremely difficult to accept and come to terms with but the fact is I was now yesterday's man. I think it was Billy Bremner who said, 'Yesterday is a long time ago in football.'

The candle had been extinguished and this time there was no going back. Everything has a beginning and everything has an end. My football career was over ...

Chapter 17

Thrown Away

I NEVER fully understood how hard transitioning out of the game would be and I think it's fair to say that the years following my enforced retirement were some of the toughest I've faced.

I did manage to play football again, albeit at a lower level in non-league for a couple of seasons, first with a team called Elmore and then Clyst Rovers. The medical advice was that my back wouldn't be able to cope with the day-to-day demands of full-time football but I'd completed my rehab and done a few runs, so in the absence of any better ideas I decided to give playing part-time a go.

A lad called Phil Lloyd, who had been a pro at Torquay United, rang me and asked if I fancied going to Elmore, just training once a week and playing on a Saturday. I was spending my days scratching around for part-time work doing deliveries, shop work or whatever else to bring in a few quid, so it provided me with an outlet and there were a few ex-pros in the team.

I got through my first match and started off there on decent money, but that was quickly slashed due to financial problems. It was another disappointment but I liked Phil so agreed to stick it out until the end of the season.

A couple of lads from the Barley Mow pub were involved with a team called Clyst Rovers so I went down there as it was a bit more local. They were managed by a lad called Dean Roberts who had also played for Exeter City. Funnily enough I'd come across Dean before. When I was at Little Lever School we did a Coca-Cola football award where you received a badge and certificate for performing different skills. There was bronze, silver and gold and Dean was on the books at Bolton Wanderers at the time. They sent a couple of players to present us with our awards and I remember him signing my certificate, which I've still got somewhere. It's strange in life how people can come back round.

I went through a season with Clyst, playing most matches. I enjoyed it to a degree but was now at a stage where I was doing it for the sake of it. When you play any sport you almost have a relationship with it and I knew in my heart of hearts I was on a downward trajectory. I'd lost a lot of my desire and love for the game and was fed up with all the disappointments. Also, when you're getting paid about £50 a match, you need a day job alongside that to survive.

I did get some coaching work through one of the lads I'd played with at Exeter called Eamonn Dolan. Eamonn had his own health battles and like me had to retire from professional football young. He'd been appointed as Exeter City's head of football in the community and was one of the few people alongside my family who truly looked out for me during that difficult period. I'll never forget that, and Eamonn, who sadly lost his life at only 48 years old, will always have a piece of my heart. I enjoyed the coaching hours but sadly it was only really in the school holidays so I needed something more substantial and regular.

I knew it was time to search for a new path so I completely retired from football around 1996 at the age of 24. Apart from the odd game of five-a-side with mates or colleagues I never really played again after that and didn't fancy just turning out at grassroots level because I needed to move my life on and find another direction.

That wasn't an easy thing to do though, and looking back I wasn't in a good place mentally because football was all I knew and I really missed it. I was struggling to come to terms with how my career had ended and didn't know what direction I wanted to go in. The door had firmly closed on me and I was battling demons while desperately trying to find some light among a lot of darkness. I wasn't an established professional player so there was little hope of landing on my feet and staying in the game with a coaching job or media work. I had a few GCSEs but I wasn't qualified in anything, and being in my mid-20s I didn't have a great deal of life experience either.

What's a professional footballer when they can't play football anymore? It's a difficult question to answer and I think upon retiring you have to face yourself, which some find harder than others. It can help open doors for you but it doesn't really matter how many trophies you've won or how good a player you've been either. A lot of players don't know themselves outside of football, as it becomes so intertwined with your identity from a young age. Retirement can be a timebomb because when it comes you lose a part of yourself.

I felt like it had been taken away from me and was resentful about how things had been handled at various stages. For all its glories and prestige, it's a cruel business where you're quickly forgotten, but it's difficult to get football out of your system. My old United team-mate Jules Maiorana was forced to retire at a similar age to me. He's said it was about seven years before he got round to watching a match again and if he'd had the option to take a chip out of his brain so he wouldn't remember any of it he'd have done so. I can understand how he felt but the problem is that it's almost impossible to escape.

Kids are playing football down the park, you walk down the street and see someone wearing a United shirt or you turn on the TV and there's a match on. It's all around you and everyone with half an interest wants to talk about it. It becomes a bit like mental torture when you don't want to think about it for a while, having had a very negative experience. You're desperate to move your life on, but you just don't know how to.

There was no aftercare or mental health support in those days for players in my situation, which led to a feeling of being isolated and on my own. I was fortunate to have the support of my family, who were fantastic, but looking back I needed some form of professional guidance to help clarify my next steps. Sadly, there was nothing forthcoming and I ended up feeling confused and afraid as I simply didn't know what to do next. I'd been given a reasonable amount of money to invest towards my future but it soon starts to whittle away and I needed someone to grab hold of me because I was lost.

I'm not bitter, life is too short for that, but I was very disappointed I didn't get more support from a game where I'd been associated with a professional club since the age of 14. You end up feeling used, surplus to requirements and thrown away. It's not surprising that the mental health of athletes often nosedives when their careers come to an end, and looking back I probably was suffering with depression. A doctor once said to me, 'An idle mind is the devil's playground,' and it's so true.

My fitness started to wane, my diet was poor and I ended up falling into bad habits such as drinking more than I should have and spending too much time in the bookies. I was used to training most days and the adrenaline rush of playing but that wasn't there anymore so naturally you look for things to replace it with, which can lead down a destructive path.

I did spend a lot of time in the pub, either through boredom or to drown my sorrows. You're trying to find solace wherever you can, even if it's through a blowout on a night out or the buzz of a win on the horses, because you're not in the best place mentally. I'd lost a bit of control as they say in psychology. I desperately needed some direction in my life because I was foggy and making bad choices. There's always a story behind people's behaviour and what's driving it. I needed time to heal and was trying to live in this carefree void, pretending everything was okay, but it was an act because inside I was really struggling.

Life was moving at an incredibly fast pace too and things were happening quickly. I stayed in Exeter until late 1996 and met a girl down there who lived in the flat opposite me. My beautiful daughter Lauren was born the following year. We got married and moved up to Doncaster but sadly it didn't work out, which was another heartbreaking thing to go through and a very sad time.

I managed to get a job with a logistics company called White Arrow doing multi-drop deliveries to bring some money in before moving on to TNT where I worked in the warehouse loading lorries, which took me up to the millennium.

Football may have moved on without me but I obviously still followed United, who were enjoying a period of unprecedented success throughout the 90s. I'd watch most matches on TV and remember the 1994 FA Cup Final win over Chelsea, then over

Liverpool two years later, but by the time of the treble in 1999 my own time at the club felt a world away – another lifetime.

I watched the Champions League Final against Bayern Munich at home while preparing to start another night shift at TNT. It was a magical night and for them to turn it around in the way they did was unbelievable. I was happy as a fan and for the lads in that team I'd known when I was there, such as Giggsy and Denis Irwin, but my life had moved on.

After my marriage split, I moved back to Bolton and continued to co-parent Lauren, seeing her every other weekend or during school holidays. I knew something in my life needed to change and in many ways Lauren was my inspiration for doing that. I wanted her to have a dad to be proud of.

I was 28 years old, back in my hometown and I'd kind of disappeared a bit after all the highs and lows of the past few years where I'd probably been dealt more than my fair share of hammer blows. Sometimes in life, though, you have to play the hand you're dealt and make the best of it. You can't sit around feeling sorry for yourself and have to keep moving forward. To quote Viktor Frankl, an Austrian psychiatrist and Holocaust survivor: 'When we are no longer able to change a situation, we are challenged to change ourselves.'

I had to accept that making a living out of professional football had gone for me and I needed to find a way to replace it constructively. The foundations needed laying again, so in 2000 I did something I'd never visualised myself doing before. I took the first step on the road to rebuilding my life and enrolled at university.

Chapter 18

Fighting Back

I STARTED university in September 2000, studying a sports science degree, after attending an open day at Bolton Institute of Higher Education, as it was then, to discuss my options. They thought it would be a good fit given my background, so I decided to give it a go.

Times were changing and degrees were starting to shape themselves around sport and other niches as well as the more traditional academic subjects. Sports science was still in its infancy but had started to creep into football with a few Premier League clubs beginning to employ its methods, including Sam Allardyce at Bolton Wanderers.

I got myself some part-time work coaching the university football team for a few hours a week and it was nice to pass on a little bit of knowledge and wisdom that I'd picked up in my relatively short time in the game. The standard was decent and it was enjoyable. I also began to progress through my coaching badges to add another string to my bow and did my 'B' licence at The Cliff in the early 2000s. It was a bit strange going back, having trained and played there so many times as a youngster.

John Barnes was on the same course and I remember the other lads joking that his badge would be in the post because realistically they weren't going to fail someone of his standing. John had recently had an unsuccessful spell as manager of Celtic and spoke about the issues he faced there with players going to the owners over his head. He said he found it hard to build unity and trust among his squad and that it was a growing problem in the modern game.

I was still exploring my options but in the end I decided that coaching wasn't a route I wanted to go down, largely due to the challenging experiences I'd had in football. It would have been a bit like someone in the military being traumatised during a war then agreeing to train the next batch of soldiers! Opportunities for full-time work also tend to be limited and it's often not a case of what you know but who you know. I understand why a lot of players go into coaching when they retire as it's a natural progression, but I knew it wasn't for me.

Going to university, however, was one of the best decisions I ever made and the first time since my football career ended that I could see a clearer path forward. I really enjoyed the course and picked up some good knowledge, not to mention new skills, such as using computer software and delivering presentations. The lecturers there, such as Andy Fallone, Paul Russell, Dave Lamb and Dan Morgan, were all absolutely outstanding.

As a mature student I was around ten years older than most of my peers and maybe didn't have some of the distractions they had because I was at a different stage of my life. It meant I could throw myself into my studies and I was elected as the course rep, where I felt I put my opinions across well.

In my third year there was an optional module to shadow a teacher in a local school for a term. I was assigned to a PE teacher who worked at a challenging school but wasn't afraid to assert his authority; he reminded me of Eric Harrison. I loved the experience so decided to do a teacher training course in further adult and higher education, which I completed in 2004.

I graduated with a 2.1, which I was absolutely over the moon about. I was in a new relationship and my beautiful son Sam was born around the same time in 2003. Life was good and it felt as if I was moving in the right direction.

I managed to land the first job I applied for, lecturing sport at Manchester College. It doesn't feel like that long ago but I seem to remember doing the presentation in the interview with acetate slides on a projector! I stayed there for 11 years, mainly delivering BTEC courses and I helped to design a degree in sports coaching in partnership with Edge Hill University, which was successful and saw us get some really good cohorts through for about four or five years. We also designed a full degree with Manchester Metropolitan University that we could run in-house, which was unique, and I was very proud of it. I also acted as a coach and mentor for other tutors and loved being around young people to help shape them and their paths into employment.

I saw a job advert for University Campus of Football Business (UCFB), a relatively new venture led by Brendan Flood, a Burnley FC executive. UCFB's unique aim was that they offered a range of degrees specific to the football industry, which obviously appealed to me. I got the job and have been there since 2015. I've really enjoyed helping young people develop their skills and have been fortunate to work alongside some fantastic academics and support staff.

One of the main selling points for the courses we run is that most of the modules are delivered pitch-side so you're in the heart of the industry. We started off at Burnley's home, Turf Moor, and have since moved to the Etihad Stadium where the facilities are incredible, although I do admit being a red working at City's ground has its challenges. I often wear my United hat walking up Joe Mercer Way just to make my presence felt! We've also moved into some cutting-edge premises around Manchester, including the use of Old Trafford for premier events, which seems a bit surreal given I played there around 30 years ago.

I've delivered modules on sports psychology, coaching, research, talent development and scouting among other things. I've done player care certificates, which have involved visits to Wembley, and we've had a couple of Premier League players on the course. It's a great job that's very rewarding and comes with a significant level of responsibility, but one of the nicest things is to bump into someone you've taught previously and hear about the exciting stuff they're up to now.

I got the bug for education so continued to progress myself academically alongside my lecturing role. I picked up a master's degree in psychology, which I finished in 2010. It was a subject that I was particularly interested in and I read a lot of theory that helped me make sense of certain experiences. As part of that I undertook some research on the use of psychological skills and imagery within professional football.

I initially applied for full funding to do my PhD but got knocked back, so decided to part-fund it myself and requested some help from the PFA, who agreed to support. They usually stop funding education for ex-professional players at master's level; however, on this occasion they stretched to help with my PhD, an incredible gesture that I can never thank them enough for. I started my PhD properly in 2015 through Liverpool John Moores University. I wanted to shine a light on the difficulties of player journeys – how they could be given more support at different stages of their careers and investigate issues such as appropriate player care (or lack of), critical moments and transitions.

The PhD was research- and study-based and you'd have regular meetings with your supervisory team to discuss progress. I had the brilliant Dr Mark Nesti, who's worked in the Premier League, as my main supervisor and also the amazing Dr Rob Morris, who's a qualified sports psychologist, as my second supervisor. The whole PhD comprised three separate studies with a total word count of 80,000 to play with.

The first and probably biggest study was an account of my own journey, looking at the culture in football at the time and some of the ups and downs that I faced. For the second study I utilised some of my contacts to interview six players who had all been involved in the game for varying lengths of time about their experiences, which threw up some interesting topics. The final study involved using some of the knowledge and information I'd acquired from the first two studies. I asked 212 former professional players via a questionnaire how issues such as injury, deselection, negative media, and not getting on with coaches and managers had affected their mental health. It was a solid-sized sample and allowed me to get closer to some ex-players who had come out of the game more recently than me.

I found bringing it all together very informative and it threw up some gaps where perhaps more support is needed. One of the main findings that surprised me was that some issues haven't changed since my time. It was good to get different views on the support available around deselection, something that I obviously experienced myself, and a topic that people on the outside will struggle to understand how tough it can be for a player, whether it's being dropped or released at the end of a contract. There can be a whole raft of reasons for it and from a psychological perspective it can affect you deeply as well as your ability to bounce back.

I undertook my viva on 6 February 2020, which is of course a very important date in the calendar of a Manchester United fan because it's the anniversary of the Munich air disaster. It made the day a little more daunting but I got through it. A viva is the oral examination that takes place at the end of a PhD and is essentially the final hurdle on the path to gaining a doctorate. It's usually done in front of three people: an internal examiner from your university, an external examiner and another who's usually more junior. The examiners have your PhD for about three months beforehand and ask you a series of critical questions. Your job is to defend your work and justify why you did things in a certain way. It was pretty gruelling in a really tight room. I was in there for four and a half hours!

Following your viva you're often given corrections to do before resubmitting your work. I had a few bits and pieces to address before getting everything signed off. I was awarded a PhD in the sports science department and it felt fantastic to finally get it all over the line. It's something I'm very proud of, a tale of redemption after the struggles I had after retiring from professional football and an important journey for me personally. The knowledge I picked up allowed me to advance my critical thinking skills and understand what had happened around my career. After several years of doing research and studying the issues I now feel qualified to help and guide other players.

I'm also glad that as a youngster I engaged with my education so that when I retired from football I had a basic level to fall back on. I was lucky to have some brilliant teachers throughout my formative years, such as Mr McFadian, Mrs Kinder, Mr Livesey and Mrs Woods, who all inspired me. I remember as an apprentice at United a lot of the other lads didn't see it as important so didn't bother turning up to college, preferring to spend their time playing pool or looking round shops. Of the 12 apprentices in our year group, only two of us passed the college course, with me being one of them.

At the time, education gave me something to concentrate on away from football and eventually that grounding helped me transition into another career. The tag of being a former professional footballer inevitably follows you around but I like to think throwing myself into my education and achieving my PhD allowed me to shed that, proving that my former career doesn't define me as a person, even though people still often ask about my experiences at Manchester United and Exeter City.

The next step for me personally could be a professorship if I decide to go down that route and maybe supervising PhDs, but I'd say my main ambition would be to pass on some of the expertise and experience I've accumulated by supporting the young players at Manchester United. It's a cause I really believe in and it would be like coming full circle. Who knows what the future holds? All I know is that I wouldn't be anywhere near as enthusiastic about working with the youngsters at Manchester City or Liverpool!

Extra Time

Chapter 19

Mental Health Matters

THE LAST few years have seen a heightened awareness of mental health in society, which can only be a good thing. It's important to talk and be open about any issues because keeping it bottled up does you no favours. Talking can help to process things, untangle potentially traumatic experiences, allowing you to see them in a different light or simply to offload. Seeking support isn't about weakness – it's for the strong to become even stronger.

It's an ongoing battle and everyone experiences it to some degree. It's also a subject that's very close to my heart after some of the trials and tribulations I've undergone on my own life's journey. Challenges come to everybody. It can be tough and things change very quickly; everything can be going brilliantly one minute then something gets thrown in your path.

The old-school attitude of not showing weakness and just getting on with it isn't very healthy because you're not expressing your feelings, which causes issues in the long run. When I was a youngster at United in that sort of environment there was no one really that you could talk to in confidence.

I remember trying to open up in a one-to-one meeting we used to have with Eric Harrison. I was feeling fatigued in the first 20 minutes of matches and nowadays a sports psychologist would diagnose that as being too nervous or overthinking the night before. The response I got was that everyone felt like that and I just needed to play through it. Everyone was tarred with the same brush and at times it felt like there was nowhere to go. It was tough and the whole experience left a mark on me as I continued through my life. I've come to learn that the greatest people listen not with their minds alone but with their hearts, minds and whole being.

In the last few years I've done some fundraising work with Manchester Mind to give something back, which gives me a great sense of fulfilment and helps you appreciate other people's struggles. I did a sponsored walk from my house in Bolton to The Cliff, continuing to Littleton Road and on to Old Trafford, which took four or five hours in total, but I managed to raise about £1,500. I also used my contacts to organise a charity golf day where we managed to get a few famous faces involved from United and elsewhere. Clarke Carlisle came and took part, a superb fella who's extremely bright and eloquent, having had his own struggles that have been well-documented. More recently I ran 50 kilometres (31 miles) to coincide with my 50th birthday, split into ten 5-kilometre runs on a treadmill each day. It's something that I enjoy doing and I would love to do more events and fundraisers in the future.

It's good to see more people talking about mental health but there's still a lot of work to do, and it's a similar story where football is concerned because it's a reflection of wider society. It can be a brutal business and you've got to be tough to survive in it for any length of time. It's not easy to make it as a professional footballer and the fact is that even by signing that first pro contract you've already got further than thousands of other lads, but really the hard work is just beginning. As a young player it's important to retain your love for the game, which is why you started playing in the first place, as your environment inevitably becomes more pressurised.

Like anything in life, hard work and dedication is crucial – extra training outside of structured sessions, working on your technique and fitness. You've got to be willing to make sacrifices and can't partake in the same things that other lads your age can freely enjoy, such as going out with your mates.

Luck is definitely a factor and there's a lot to be said for being in the right place at the right time. Moments can be massive, because if you come on and score the winner it can set your career on a different path.

Mental strength and resilience are key attributes. Traditionally football is a very macho environment where players can be treated like objects rather than human beings. You've got to be tough mentally to handle the level of scrutiny where players can be crucified for a single mistake. It's not easy to deal with the peaks and troughs of a career and, trust me, there are a lot more downs than ups.

Self-belief is vital and probably something I lacked at times during my own career. A lot of the top players have that level of confidence almost built into them to the point where it's unshakeable. If you look at Gary and Phil Neville, both had brilliant careers not because of their ability but because they were extremely driven and headstrong. They were ruthless enough to win the right to play then stay there. If I'd had their mentality maybe I'd have gone further, but then you've also got to stay true to yourself.

Football can be cruel and the extremes are ridiculous. Careers can be very fragile and it's often not about how good you are but who sees your worth. There's a certain coldness to it. In life you just want to be loved and valued, which you don't really get in the industry, so it's not surprising that it can create mental health issues.

As a player you naturally experience a lot of anxiety for a multitude of reasons. You worry about your form, place in the team, getting injured, and you're always looking for clues as to whether the manager rates you. There's a lot of insecurity, particularly at lower levels, and you're not always in charge of your own destiny. Players are often on short-term contracts and if your club doesn't want you anymore or decides to sell you the rug is pulled from under your feet. I had to relocate 250 miles to Exeter to attempt to continue my career after being released by United, which was stressful and a big deal, but there will be players with families who are forced to do it every year or two. Their kids will have to move school and it can put a huge strain on relationships.

Like everyone, players are often dealing with personal issues. The likes of Paul Gascoigne, Paul Merson, Keith Gillespie and Paul McGrath all performed at an incredibly high level during their careers in an era where there was a distinct lack of support for mental health issues. What's happening off the field can impact you on it – they say happy players are better players and there's some truth in that.

When I played there was a lot of undiagnosed mental health issues in the game that just weren't spoken about, and most coaches weren't really bothered as long as their players did the business on a Saturday. The problem is that has a masking effect, then the shit hits the fan when players retire and are on their own. The immediate period after I was forced to retire was the most difficult of my life. I was left with nothing. It was as though I'd never played and there was no support whatsoever for my psychological state.

Football closed the door on me and nobody stepped forward with any kind of guidance.

I was lucky in a way that eventually I could choose to go in another direction but a lot really struggle with the transition or never fully recover. I think the data from the PFA shows something like three out of five players' marriages end after they retire, which is remarkable when you think about it but maybe not totally surprising. There are also several former footballers who have spent time within the prison system because they've chosen poorly, trying to replace the thrill and lifestyle that football gave them.

Unfulfillment can be another issue and one I can relate to. A lot of former pros feel they didn't achieve their ambitions because as a kid you dream of winning league titles, cup finals or playing for England, but it doesn't happen for many. If you have regrets or there's a question mark over your career it can be difficult to live with.

I think the game is making a concerted effort with mental health awareness and generally being more inclusive. There's more opportunity now to speak out but often the green shoots of progress are tempered by the fact that a lot of the issues are hidden or swept under the carpet.

The Blackpool player Jake Daniels became the first openly gay British footballer since Justin Fashanu in 2022, which was a massive moment, but there must be a lot more who don't come out for fear of the repercussions. There was also the tragic story of Jeremy Wisten, who took his own life following his release by Manchester City, so we still have a lot to learn, especially when it comes to the treatment of young players.

I'd like to see mental health support given to youngsters in academies straight away when they come in at nine or ten to help prepare them for what they're going to come up against. Kids start playing football because they completely enjoy it, but if they start to show ability and get picked up by clubs it can become too serious too young, often denying them the chance to play with their mates or grassroots team. You see kids of 11 or 12 doing contract signings or going on tours in their club tracksuits. It seems to me that this is early professionalisation, which can give them a false impression they've made it. It's so important for them to have a balanced identity and other interests so they're not putting all their eggs in one basket with football, which is something that you do, not who you are.

I'm not saying remove the right to dream but just manage it more effectively. It can be a status thing for parents, who get carried away, and there needs to be more education provided on how to manage their child's expectations because not many will make it as professional footballers. Their heads can get turned then they start thinking a million miles into the future and about the extrinsic rewards, which puts more pressure on the child.

The academy structure now is completely different to what I knew as a young player and there are a lot of positives to it such as the increased emphasis on education. Historically, lads like me who were academically bright tended to struggle with the nature of the YTS system, whereas lads who had maybe had a bit of turbulence in their upbringing and were more streetwise seemed to survive it better, so it's good to see that changing.

There are also numerous progressive and interesting ideas being employed across different clubs. I've heard that Manchester City now give all young players a two-year apprenticeship at 16 followed by a three-year pro deal through to 21, which is a game-changer as it gives them a level of security and a proper go at it while allowing for late developers. Some lads need patience to allow them to grow and develop, but a lot don't get it.

I guess the danger is it could be kicking the can down the road and maybe delaying the inevitability of deselection. Young players are vulnerable at a club up until they're established in the first team because ultimately you're expendable prior to that. It's one thing to get into a first team but it's even more difficult to stay there for a sustained period, and that's where a lot of youngsters end up coming unstuck.

Crystal Palace were one of the first clubs to provide any sort of aftercare to players who have been released from their academy. It's a pioneering idea and it will be interesting to see how it develops. The flip side is who wants to be involved with a club that's just broken your heart? Sometimes it's better to move on. I think there's potentially a lot of value in the aftercare concept but it needs auditing across all the clubs employing it to give a truer picture. It would be interesting to talk to some players who have been through it to get their thoughts on whether they've received the best possible care. There's a lot of masking that goes on and is passed off as solutions to problems.

It's a topic I'm passionate about, having experienced the heartbreak of deselection in my own career. Being released by United was a brutal experience that affected me deeply so it gives me a sense of purpose to try to help young players who have been through something similar. When you consider it was a neighbour who got me a trial with Exeter, maybe United could have done a lot more. I often wonder what happened to some of the other lads in our youth team who also got released, and where they ended up.

It's hard to say what the answers are but I think there needs to be a plan or structure in place for all players of all ages when they come out of the game, a path they can trust and follow that also meets their emotional needs, providing mental health support if required. I'd also like to see the PFA sending out more brochures featuring case studies of players who have retired young and the path they've followed. For most, all they've ever known is football so they lack transferrable skills due to having no experience of life outside it. Next steps after retiring are often not considered until one day it hits them in the face.

We're starting to see jobs being advertised for player care officers employed specifically to look after players' well-being and it's nice to help to drive that in my lecturing role, where we deliver the courses for it. It's a good opportunity, given the growth of mental health provision, to understand what players go through and how to provide the relevant support.

I went out to Miami with UCFB, who have a range of incredible hubs around the world. I visited Inter Miami, which is a superb set-up, and youth development in Major League Soccer is definitely progressing. The American sports model is very much built on a dual career, with players selected or drafted after they've come out of the college system and done a degree. In the UK it's the opposite but things are beginning to change. Diverse influences have advanced things such as religious understanding and spirituality. I've read a couple of books on transcendence and chaplaincy in sport, which is an interesting topic and provides a great source of meaning to some athletes that helps to keep them grounded.

The whole thing is a work in progress, not just in football but in professional sport. We'll always need decent people with good values who players can speak to in confidence without judgement. A lot of players are still reluctant to talk about issues they may have because they're worried that any sign of perceived weakness will mean not getting picked on a Saturday. I know some clubs have employed methods that include players registering their mood before training on an iPad, where they have to click on faces ranging from happy to sad. I've heard it said that all the players will just tap the happy face regardless of how they're feeling to avoid any scrutiny on their place in the team.

There's a difference between mental health issues and mental illness, although they can be connected. If you have mental health issues it doesn't mean you can't function and perform at a high level but there's still a stigma that players who speak out about the way they're feeling are weak, which then leads to them becoming very introverted as they just try to survive.

Managers often have different priorities but we're starting to see more modern, forward-thinking coaches coming through such as Jürgen Klopp, Eddie Howe and Brendan Rodgers. Brendan gets a lot of praise for his persona and way of dealing with people. He managed Liverpool but was at United as a youngster on trial for a short time and knew Adrian Doherty from growing up in Northern Ireland. The right sort of characters who are more people-friendly are beginning to appear in the game at the highest level but it will take time to trickle down and we need more of them.

We've made progress since my time but a lot of similar issues remain. I think overall things are improving but football as an industry still has much to learn.

Chapter 20

The Modern Game

THE ESTABLISHMENT of the Premier League changed football forever and the resultant influx of money has made it unrecognisable from the game I knew growing up. Modern players are a different breed; the money they earn and lifestyles they lead means there's a disconnect with the fans, which is only growing. I imagine living in the public eye isn't easy and there can be a lot of hangers-on who don't have their best interests at heart, which leads to them withdrawing because they don't know who to trust. My childhood heroes such as Bryan Robson and Norman Whiteside would often socialise with supporters and were generally more accessible but it's not the same now, sadly.

I'm a great advocate for players at the top of the game reaping the rewards but I'm not a fan of rewarding mediocrity. When you watch the Premier League, you often see poor-quality play such as frequently giving the ball away or failing to get a cross past the first man, and these lads are earning six figures every week. Salaries often don't correlate to performance and contracts aren't really earned as much these days, where clubs hand them out to protect a player's resale value.

Money can be a destructive thing; it kills the fire and determination in young players to keep improving when they're awarded long-term contracts on big wages often before they're even established in the first team. As the saying goes, there's no hunger in paradise, and Eric Harrison used to tell us as youngsters at United that you're nothing in football until you've made 100 appearances at a club.

Players are now far more powerful than they were in my time, which creates its own set of problems. The majority seem to have agents from a young age, which I think a lot of clubs regard as a nuisance, although I do see the value in them. Youngsters coming through academies need to build mental strength and resilience but youth football seems to have gone from the cruel harsh world that I experienced to the dial being turned completely the other way and total opulence.

I think young people in general today are a lot more fragile and superficial than those of previous generations and too many in the modern world are quick to blame others for their failings. I often try to drive home to students the importance of self-responsibility. You get out of things what you put in, but the rise of social media and reality TV has led to some people thinking they can achieve a nice lifestyle without having to work hard because they idolise bad role models. Sometimes you need a bollocking or a bit of adversity to enable you to grow but it must be a nightmare for coaches who can't be totally honest with their players for fear of repercussions or them throwing their toys out of the pram. I've heard a few coaches say that they love football but hate the industry and I can understand why.

Coaching is another area of the game that needs more scrutiny as a lot of modern players are very robotic in their play due to being over-coached. There's so much analysis now, which can disrupt development and prevent a player from having any sort of individuality. We live in a very visual world where everything is observable and technology can become another tool to focus too much on the negatives such as positioning or mistakes. How can you expect players to feel confident enough to express themselves when they're constantly being lectured on the things they're doing wrong?

Performance analysis is conducted in great depth but it needs to show how to win football matches first and foremost. Football is a very simple game that's often complicated. When the golfer Jack Nicklaus was in his prime he said that all he needed from his caddy was the distance and to be told he was the best player in the world. We're obsessed with measuring everything and sometimes less can be more.

We're also starting to see the use of virtual reality technology creep in but sometimes the simple methods such as knocking a ball against a wall can be just as, if not more, effective. It does hold some benefit such as reducing the number of times youngsters head the ball following the rising evidence that it can lead to dementia in later life. It's scary now when you think that we used to practise headers in training pretty much every day when I was at United and often repetitively as part of drills or shape work.

There's still room for improvement in the standard of coaching, particularly in the messaging that young players receive. They're often given feedback such as 'improve forward play around the box' but are never shown how to do it. Lots of instructions are given out but there's no real teaching behind it, which is poor coaching. I think it was Johan Cruyff who said that more teachers are needed in football.

Too many coaches are in the game for the wrong reasons. We need proper football people who have played the game at a reasonable level and have a genuine love for it as opposed to those who are just in it for the money or the status it gives them. In wider society these days we seem to recruit on knowledge and charisma alone, with actual skills and values coming last when really it should be the other way around. People need to have the right intentions, otherwise it causes carnage – get the culture right and grow from that.

The ways of consuming media around the game have changed drastically with the rise of social media platforms. It all probably started around 15 years ago with Facebook and then Twitter, which followed a couple of years later. I remember deciding to join the latter and because of my previous association with United and Exeter City I started to attract a few followers, which took me aback. There's a lot of positives and it's nice to engage with other fans as it provides the opportunity to share views and opinions. I get some nice interactions when I post old pictures of my playing days and it's also allowed me to reconnect with former team-mates and reminisce. People use it in different capacities, with some being very active and others not so much. You can promote your work or attract wider support for a particular cause because the footprint goes a lot further, and a single tweet can be seen by thousands of people all over the world.

I think modern players' social media is often directly linked to their brand and getting their message out there. I don't know how much attention they actually pay to it. In truth it's probably better they stay away from it and concentrate on their football. Players often use it in two parts and a lot of it is driven by their social media managers. You'll see them post something fairly generic after a win and following a loss they'll be saying they need to do better, or the obligatory 'we go again next week' tweet. There have been quite a few of those posts from United players in the last few years!

Sadly, there can be a darker side to social media. The vast majority of people are really nice and respectful but you do get the odd idiot every so often. The level of abuse that can be directed at players when things aren't going well often goes beyond criticism of their performances to levels that are downright unacceptable. An example of this is the racist abuse directed at Marcus Rashford, Jadon Sancho and Bukayo Saka following England's defeat on penalties to Italy in the final of Euro 2020.

I think everyone has experienced the negative side of social media at some point and the fact that people don't have to use their actual name to create accounts brings a degree of anonymity that reduces the chances of there being consequences for their behaviour. It's quite sinister because trolls will hide behind an alias to direct abuse, which can cause mental health issues for the recipient and at times be bordering on harassment. When you're on the end of something like that you can spend time and a lot of negative energy trying to work out who it is and why they're doing it. It's often born of jealousy for some reason or the person not being happy with their own life so they think they can have a go at others. I think it was Aristotle who said, 'The only way to avoid criticism is to say nothing, do nothing and be nothing.'

You also have to be careful about what you post because it can come back to haunt you, sometimes even affecting your employment or future job prospects. Overall, I enjoy the whole experience but think that more regulation needs to be brought in from the social media companies to help combat some of the issues.

A lot of things nowadays are done to attract likes and followers, and too few people seem to be courageous enough to just be themselves. It can be a fickle world where individuals carry the most power, and fancams are another phenomenon who have tried to tap into that in the last few years. They're held on a pedestal by some fans as though they know everything because they've got thousands of followers despite most of them talking rubbish week in, week out. The culture it's created is centred on opinions that are the lowest form of knowledge. Empathy is the highest and I often think that former players are better placed to give insight or comment because they've actually lived it.

'Watch-alongs' are an interesting idea and I admire them for their creativity and ability to perform. It can be very lucrative when you start getting things like advertising involved but there's also a lot of agendas that get pushed on to gullible people and this creates division within fanbases, feeding into that toxic social media culture. I think some of them almost want their team to lose or certain players to have a nightmare because they know it will result in more clicks and interactions.

I used to buy *Red Issue* outside Old Trafford on matchdays, which I guess was the sort of equivalent of its time. I'd walk into the players' lounge with my copy in my back pocket and a lot of the first-team lads would be wanting to read it because they'd see the humour in it. Personally, fancamming isn't for me but I see why there's a niche for it. The more traditional mediums still hold value and there's some really good content out there rather than just views and opinions.

I've had the opportunity to get involved with a bit of media work over the years, which I've really enjoyed. I was invited on to *Red Wednesday* by Bill Rice, Liam Bradford and Sarah Collins, which was a midweek show broadcast on BBC Radio Manchester and featured quite regularly for a couple of years. It was a taster of something a little bit different for me and nice as a fan to be able to discuss all things United with people such as Rowetta from the Happy Mondays. From there I got an opportunity with BBC Radio Devon, who were looking for someone based in the Manchester area with a connection to Exeter City. Luckily, that would be me – there's not many of us about! They asked me to do some summarising for a league match at Macclesfield Town so I agreed to give it a go without really knowing what to expect. I turned up at Moss Rose and made my way to the commentary position. It was a strange coincidence for my first match to be at the same ground where Joe Brown, the youth development officer at Manchester United, had approached me about going on trial so many years before. My colleague on the night, Anthony Wareing, who I've since worked with a lot, was a superstar and really helped me through it.

I loved it and have never looked back since. Any time Exeter are playing in the north I do the co-commentary. I also got the opportunity to work on a couple of United matches, against Watford and Tranmere in the FA Cup, for Radio Manchester with Liam Bradford, which was an amazing experience.

There's an art to it but you do improve with practice. You have to be very mindful of the fact that listeners can't see what's going on so it's your job to paint the picture of what's happening on the pitch. For example, when a player crosses the ball into the box you have to be more descriptive and use words like fizzed, drilled, curled, swept or floated. It takes a little getting used to but, as well as Anthony Wareing, I work with some absolutely brilliant lads at Radio Devon, including Alan Richardson, James

Vickery, Mark Edwards, Ollie Heptinstall, Anthony Pilling and Jim Dale, who I'm in awe of as media professionals. I've learned something from them all.

The present-day Exeter City team are really good to watch too. They achieved promotion from League Two at the end of 2021/22 after knocking on the door for the previous few years and I was made up for them. It's nice to see the club doing well, as they have a very good record of developing young players, like United, and a lot of the current squad have come through the ranks. The challenge now is to establish themselves in League One, which they seem to be on track for, having recorded a mid-table finish in their first season.

It's great to still have a connection with the club and I had the opportunity to go back in the summer of 2021 to play in a veterans' match against Tiverton Town. We got to have a look round St James Park, which had changed a lot since I was last there 25 years before, and all the memories came flooding back. It was nice to catch up with a few people who I hadn't seen for a long time too.

The temptation to get back out there and play one more time was too much to resist. You think you can still do it and run around like you did when you were 20 but the reality is that age catches up. We ended up losing 1-0, which wasn't bad considering our opponents were a lot younger than us and most of our lads were out of condition or carrying a bit of extra timber. I lasted about 20 minutes; my fitness was okay because I'd done quite a lot of running in the build-up but that doesn't help you mimic the movements your body has to do in a game of football, which I'd not done for a long time. It was all over for me when I chased one of their lads down the wing and he stopped and went again. As I pushed off for the second time I felt my Achilles tendon splinter, which meant I had my foot in a bucket of ice all night and it was very painful for a few weeks afterwards.

I returned to Exeter for the Devon derby in April 2023, just over 30 years since I played in it. It was an enjoyable trip and the club really looked after me. I did a question-and-answer session in hospitality before the match as well as some bits with the media guys Scott Palfrey, Zandie Thornton and Craig Bratt for the club website. They're fantastic lads, as are Jed Penberthy and Harrison Lane, who I also get on really well with. It was also great to catch up with Stuart James, who's a brilliant bloke, and the BBC's Hamish Marshall, who I last met when he was interviewing me around 30 years ago!

Exeter City is a fantastic football club that has a special place in my heart and holds some great memories. It was very humbling to have a few diehard fans coming over for a chat who remembered seeing me play. Sadly, the result didn't go in our favour on the day, with Plymouth triumphing 1-0, although to be fair they were a very good team who ended up winning League One that season.

It was something I'd always wanted to do. I'm so glad I did it and hopefully there will be another opportunity to go back in the future. The club and football in general have changed dramatically since I played but it's the same game I loved as a kid growing up and it's a pleasure to still be involved in some capacity.

Chapter 21

From Red to Read

WHEN I look back at it now, my life has been split into two halves. The first is my football career, then I've spent almost the last quarter of a century involved in education in various capacities.

Some might say I've been through a lot and battled adversity at various points but I have so much to be grateful for and I'm always able to count on the support of my family. The good values instilled by my parents have helped me a lot on the journey and, when I reflect upon my early years, I'm always proud to recall their work ethic, sacrifices and unconditional love that they demonstrated. I was extremely fortunate to experience a secure, loving home and nothing ever being too much trouble for them, which has continued throughout my life.

I've always been close to my sister Jan, who's four years younger than me and such a beautiful person. She currently works in a primary school caring for children with special educational needs. Jan has an incredible son, Nathan, who has autism. His courage and fight to deal with the adversity life has given him lifts and inspires me every day.

My twin brother Kev was always one of my biggest supporters. He tragically passed away from sepsis in October 2020 at the age

201

of just 48, which was a massive shock. Kev was born deaf and overcame a lot of challenges throughout his life. He was more of an observer who enjoyed watching sport, and when I was at United he'd often be on the touchline with my dad. We were close and losing him rocked our whole family to the core. I always say you never know what's coming tomorrow so it's important to just try to be happy in each moment and take nothing for granted.

My uncle Jim, who's also sadly no longer with us, always took a keen interest in my football career and would often come to watch me play, with my cousins Ian and Stuart. He was another huge Manchester United fan who had been going to Old Trafford with my dad since they were young and was good friends with former player and coach Jim Ryan.

I've been blessed with two wonderful children – my daughter Lauren and son Sam. I'm so proud of them both. Lauren is in her mid-20s now and works as a speech and language therapist for the NHS. She's a superstar and has always been very academic. She did superbly well in her GCSEs and A-Levels before completing an English degree at Newcastle University, followed by two master's degrees, one in linguistics and the other in speech and language therapy. She's doing incredibly well for herself despite experiencing a huge scare in 2023 when she suffered a stroke at only 25 years old. It came from nowhere and was a very upsetting time for all the family. Fortunately she's made a fantastic recovery and just 16 weeks later ran the Great North Run half-marathon to raise funds for the British Heart Foundation, something that took lots of courage and resilience and was an epic achievement.

Sam is another superstar and is in his early 20s, now. Initially he went down the football route as part of Oldham Athletic's academy. He showed a lot of promise but sadly, like many young players, didn't get the breaks he deserved. He now works as a community sport activator where he runs soccer schools for Bolton Wanderers and coaches the younger age groups. He's really enjoying it and they've just put him through his level-one and level-two coaching badges so it's looking likely that's the route he'll end up going down career-wise. I always echo Sir Matt Busby's words at Blue Stars to him: 'As long as you're enjoying yourself, that's the main thing.'

Manchester United continue to play a big part in my life and will always be my club. Erik ten Hag seems to have made a decent start and doesn't suffer fools gladly, which is good, but the last decade has been difficult since the gaffer retired, as we've lived largely off reputation. It's even more frustrating when you see what our neighbours Manchester City have achieved in that time. It's a different ideology as they've thrown a lot of money at it but they're leaving us behind and it's sad to see.

I don't agree one bit with the ownership of the Glazer family, who put the club in a lot of debt when they bought it in 2005, which remains a heavy financial burden to this day. Old Trafford needs refurbishment, as does the training ground, which was cutting-edge when it first opened. From a fan's perspective, they haven't been a good thing for Manchester United. Their time is up and they need to depart to allow the club to move forward. They're simply not bothered about the club or the fans but, who knows, by the time this book is published they may have sold up and moved on. We can only hope anyway.

I got involved with the Association of Former Manchester United Players in about 2010. A good friend, Ian Brunton, who used to watch me as a youngster, rang me when I was working at Manchester College and asked whether I'd like to get involved with the Manchester United ex-players' association, which I knew nothing about. He passed my details on to Paddy Crerand, who funnily enough I bumped into not long after in the Old Nags Head pub. I had a chat about it with Paddy, who's a top man, and he said he'd be in touch. True to his word Paddy left a message on my mobile later that night, letting me know that my details had been passed on to David Sadler, who was in charge at the time, and verified everything. I've been involved ever since and I'm extremely proud indeed to be a member.

The association is set up to support former players and raise money for charity, which is brilliant. The first event I was invited to was a golf day at Northenden where my team just missed out on winning by a point, but we were given a nice crystal jug that had been made to celebrate 25 years of Sir Alex managing the club. The gaffer came and played in the tournament and there was a good turnout.

Since then I've been to most of the events. They hold two golf days a year and there's a reunion dinner in April where it's always nice to catch up with a few old team-mates and meet players from different eras, including the likes of Carlo Sartori, Paddy Crerand, Wilf McGuinness, Mickey Thomas and Lou Macari, who are all brilliant people. I've met Denis Law a couple of times, who's such a top-class fella and has time for everybody as well as being one of the greatest centre-forwards that Britain has ever produced.

I sat next to Tony Hawksworth at one of the events, who was the goalkeeper when the Busby Babes won the FA Youth Cup in 1956. It was fascinating to hear him talk about Duncan Edwards and how unbelievable he was. Tony said Duncan could play at centre-half and run the show or do the same from centre-forward. It's quite special to be included in the list of names when you look at the programme for each event, and I'm proud of my association with the club.

I've also been very fortunate to get to know the United historian and author Roy Cavanagh MBE. He once sent me one of his books and had written inside, 'To someone who has worn the red shirt', which made me feel truly humbled. Roy also had a contact up at Bishop Auckland called Steve Newcomb. Bishop Auckland, of course, has a strong connection with Manchester United, having sent three of their players to help the club in the aftermath of the tragic Munich air disaster in 1958. There were genuine fears that with a severely depleted squad United would go under and, put simply, if they hadn't sent those players to help bolster the ranks I may not have had the chance to spend five years at the club I love more than three decades later.

Steve invited us up there for an event that I was delighted to attend. Roy spoke about the players that Bishop had sent, before I talked about my journey and also around some of the highs and lows that football throws at you. Incredibly, afterwards they asked me to write some thoughts on a 1958 commemorative plaque, which I was absolutely bowled over by. I wrote the poem below and I'm truly thankful to Bishop Auckland for this amazing honour.

> *To help Utd rise,*
> *3 players were sent,*
> *No words will convey,*
> *What this truly meant*

I left the club over three decades ago but people always want to talk about it, and in a weird way the interest seems to grow the older I get. I'm in my early 50s now but fans still want to know about anything from Fergie or Giggsy to what Adrian Doherty was like.

My life has moved on, of course, but I often get taken back there, and other people sometimes seem to know more about my time at United than I do.

I even get some post through occasionally with the request to sign photo cards, and the letters always make me smile. I get asked to jump on podcasts from time to time and I've featured on one with Clint Boon from the Inspiral Carpets, which was a particular thrill. I've done interviews with esteemed journalists such as Oliver Kay and Ian Herbert and for fan magazines of both United and Exeter City, which is incredibly humbling as I was only in the professional game for a relatively short spell.

In recent times, I've been invited to share some experiences with young footballers based around the psychological skills needed to become a professional player. Salford City's director of football, Chris Casper, and the owner of a touring company, Rob Hope, regularly invite me to speak to groups of Japanese players at Hotel Football. I've also been asked to talk about mental health to young age-group players at a company called Select Soccer run by the former Bolton Wanderers player Andy Mason. I truly enjoy imparting some wisdom and hope I can help them in some small way.

I was a reasonably good footballer who got to a decent level with some solid achievements – playing for United reserves at 16, the first-team Histon friendly at 17, captaining a Football League team at the same age, then playing in the Football League with Exeter City. However, the injury I suffered meant my potential was sadly never fulfilled or realised. I think with the way it worked out it's natural to feel a tinge of disappointment when I reflect on it but I must remember that there were plenty of good times too.

My football journey included some brilliant experiences, but it's just a shame it didn't go how I wanted it to, and often in life reality doesn't meet the expectation. A lot of people from the outside only see the glamour and not the deselection, injuries, negative media, managers screaming at you and having to perform under pressure. I loved football but I didn't like what the industry was at times, and some of it never truly felt right for me.

On reflection, it was a blessing in disguise. There's a Latin phrase, *ex malo bonum*, which means 'out of bad comes good', that sums it up well. Investing time in my education allowed me to balance my life out a bit more as I moved away from football. One of the things I'm most proud of is how I got back up and moved on, because it takes a lot of character and resilience.

The boxing trainer Brendan Ingle once said, 'Be kind to people on your way up, because you'll meet them again on your way back down.' Great advice and so true.

Ultimately football was something I did, not who I am. There's more to life and I've always had other interests even when I was playing. The work I do for Manchester Mind gives me huge satisfaction and fulfilment. I enjoy my golf and hit the ball quite well. At the time of writing, I play off a generous 18 handicap and wish I could get out there more. I also like a bit of horse racing, which is maybe a result of all those afternoons spent in the bookies after training when I was at Exeter!

I did balloon up in weight at one stage, largely due to my mental state and battling some demons. In recent times, though, I've focused on keeping on top of my fitness, which in turn helps with my mental health. I try to get some runs in a few times a week at the gym and feel better for it. I always try to keep how I'm feeling to around seven or eight out of ten because I know I can deal with that. The philosophy is simple. Ten out of ten never lasts and a low score needs to be snapped out of quickly – never too high, never too low.

My story is one of ups and downs, showing that life is rarely a straightforward journey and often doesn't work out how you expect it to. Everybody has highs and lows, good and bad times, but it's how you deal with those that matters. Be gracious and humble in your achievements and battle hard through your disappointments. The brilliant Rudyard Kipling advised us to treat the impostors of winning and losing in the same way.

I had my PhD graduation in July 2022. It was a really special day and allowed me to cement the journey of 'From Red to Read' nicely. It underlined that I'd progressed my education to an advanced level and I don't suppose there's many people out there who have played professional football for Manchester United then gone on to obtain a PhD. I'm probably unique in that respect.

I strongly believe that everything happens for a reason and there's a lot of destiny in life. My advice to anyone who's struggling or feels like they've been dealt a blow that has turned their world upside down is to never give up and always search for light within darkness. I lost my professional football career at the age of 22, had screws and plates inserted into my spine and was forced to go down another path, but life isn't about what happens to you, it's about how you react to what happens to you.

As Ernest Hemingway said, 'A man can be destroyed but not defeated.'

It's certainly been a journey. If anyone asks what I was like as a footballer my response is always that I got man of the match away at Stoke City, on a cold, windy, muddy night. That's the true measure of a player, so they say.

However, at my PhD graduation I remember telling my son and daughter what I truly felt within that moment: 'How you both remember me as a person is this – from a fight I couldn't win, I got back up again.'

Dr Alan Tonge

This poem has helped me through at times over the years and I've found great meaning from it. It's called 'If' by Rudyard Kipling, which he wrote to guide his son on the difficult and challenging issues thrown up during the journey of life.

If you can keep your head when all about you
Are losing theirs and blaming it on you,
If you can trust yourself when all men doubt you,
But make allowance for their doubting too;
If you can wait and not be tired by waiting,
Or being lied about, don't deal in lies,
Or being hated, don't give way to hating,
And yet don't look too good, nor talk too wise:

If you can dream – and not make dreams your master;
If you can think – and not make thoughts your aim;
If you can meet with Triumph and Disaster
And treat those two impostors just the same;
If you can bear to hear the truth you've spoken
Twisted by knaves to make a trap for fools,
Or watch the things you gave your life to, broken,
And stoop and build 'em up with worn-out tools:

If you can make one heap of all your winnings
And risk it on one turn of pitch-and-toss,
And lose, and start again at your beginnings
And never breathe a word about your loss;
If you can force your heart and nerve and sinew
To serve your turn long after they are gone,
And so hold on when there is nothing in you
Except the Will which says to them: 'Hold on!'

If you can talk with crowds and keep your virtue,
Or walk with Kings – nor lose the common touch,
If neither foes nor loving friends can hurt you,
If all men count with you, but none too much;
If you can fill the unforgiving minute
With sixty seconds' worth of distance run,
Yours is the Earth and everything that's in it,
And – which is more – you'll be a Man, my son!

Penalties

Chapter 22

If I Could Play One More Time

FOR A bit of fun to end the book, I've picked a combined Manchester United and Exeter City team from my former team-mates.

It's an interesting concept and is important to note that these aren't necessarily the best players I played with during my time at both clubs but those who had the biggest impact on me. Inevitably there are some great footballers in there and some real characters too. Not to mention plenty of big drinkers!

I had to pick myself and, in the interests of balance, I've gone for five players each from United and Exeter so here goes …

Manager – Alan Ball

Perhaps a controversial one to start.

If you were to compare the managerial CVs of Sir Alex Ferguson and Alan Ball there would only be one winner. Fergie is probably the greatest manager of all time but I've got to go for Bally, who had a bigger impact on my career.

He gave me an opportunity to play first-team football after I'd been released by United when I could easily have drifted out of the game, and I'll always be grateful for that. He was a legend and as manager of this lot he'd teach the players a thing or two in five-a-side before hosting plenty of team-bonding sessions down the pub after training.

Goalkeeper – Kevin Miller

I was lucky enough to play with some great keepers across different levels. I've known Micky Pollitt since grassroots football; we signed for United together and he went on to have a great career. At United, Les Sealey was completely mad and Gary Walsh was a decent keeper who was unlucky with injuries. Mark Bosnich was a brilliant shot-stopper who arguably enjoyed his best years at Aston Villa but holds the distinction of being the only player that Fergie signed twice.

I've got to go with Kev Miller though, who was our goalkeeper at Exeter. When I first arrived at the club, Kev was one of the lads that I stayed in digs with and he had a great personality. They say all goalkeepers are a bit mad but I think in a way they have to be to dive at players' feet on cold mornings or come for crosses with centre-forwards trying to batter them.

He was a proper goalkeeper, a good shot-stopper; however, what stood out about him is how comfortable he was with the ball at his feet at a time when most keepers weren't. Pitches weren't great in those days but if he had to deal with the ball being played back to him or long throw-ins into the box, Kev could handle it all, no problem. He could kick with both feet as well as being very vocal, with a big presence in the goal.

Kev played non-league before he was given an opportunity at Exeter and got a decent move to Birmingham City. He later played in the Premier League with Crystal Palace and racked up a few hundred appearances over the course of his career. He's now come full circle in his role as goalkeeping coach back at Exeter and it's been nice to bump into him at a few matches when I've been doing the radio commentary. A top lad.

Right-back – Scott Hiley

There were a few strong candidates for this spot. Viv Anderson won two European Cups under Brian Clough at Nottingham Forest and was an experienced head by the time he wound up at United later in his career. Micky Duxbury had a great career, making hundreds of appearances for Manchester United, and Lee Martin will always hold the distinction of scoring the winning goal for the club in an FA Cup Final.

But I've gone for another Exeter City team-mate – Scott Hiley. Scott was a very good technical player with pace, who could also operate in a more attacking role. At the time there wasn't much pressure on full-backs to bomb on and attack, with the emphasis more on defending, but he could do both. He'd whip crosses into the box and scored some good goals too.

He was probably the reason I ended up playing in midfield for Exeter because he had the right-back spot absolutely nailed down. It was a very difficult task to get in front of him. I think he was injured when I made my debut and I played behind him in a match at Reading where he scored the perfect hat-trick.

He was a humble lad who didn't really say a lot but could hold his own with the banter. When you're a key member of the squad as he was you don't need to crow really. He also got a move to Birmingham City and I believe he later played for Bally again during a spell at Manchester City before returning to Exeter later in his career.

Centre-half – Paul McGrath

Another tough one. I was lucky enough to play a couple of times alongside Steve Bruce, who was a brilliant centre-half for Manchester United and cornerstone of the first great team that Sir Alex built. I also played with Derek Brazil and Jason Lydiate in the reserves and junior teams, who were both good lads and had decent careers. Jon Brown at Exeter would be another rock-solid choice.

For my first pick I've got to go with Paul McGrath, who was captain when I made my debut for United reserves against West Brom. I was only 16 so it was a surreal experience to play alongside him at the Theatre of Dreams, and pretty special really.

Paul is a beautiful person, a complete gentle giant who was battling demons that few were aware of at the time. A Rolls-Royce of a centre-half who was world-class on his day and probably one of the best to play for the club.

He probably played his best football for Aston Villa after being written off by United and featured prominently in two World Cups for his native Republic of Ireland, where they regard him as a legend.

Centre-half – Peter Whiston

A classy operator to partner Paul in defence. Peter was a ball-playing centre-half before it was fashionable. A nice player who would win his battles but could play as well.

Peter was a good pro with a slender build and a bit of a milk-bottle complexion. He was a decent aerial threat, which was illustrated when he nodded home from my cross in the Devon derby.

He was from Widnes but, like me, had made his way down south, and Bally ended up signing him for Southampton when he got the job there too. A bright lad and maybe not your stereotypical footballer because he had other educational interests outside the game. I believe he's a financial advisor now.

Left-back – Dave Cooper

The obvious choice for this position is Denis Irwin, who was at United the last season I was there in 1990/91. Andy Cook at Exeter was a good player, as was Clayton Blackmore, who was a great servant to Manchester United.

But I had to go for my mate Coops, which he'll be over the moon about. We've had some great times together. My best mate in football, he was a proper character who enjoyed a drink and was daft as a brush. We lived in digs together and he was always in among the banter.

As a player he was a warrior who gave everything, and a good tackler. Like me he had quite a short career, which was pretty much ended by a horrific leg break sustained playing for Exeter reserves while going for a 50/50 ball. It was one of those horrible ones where, because there was nobody in the stands, you clearly heard the sickening sound of it snapping, like a tree branch. He needed to have a rod inserted down his shin and I think he did come back from it for a while but it was a big blow for him.

I'm still in touch with him and he's a youth coach at Crystal Palace now.

Right wing – John Hodge

There's a few in the frame for this one. Adrian Doherty was absolutely brilliant as a youngster at United before injury halted his progress. Andrei Kanchelskis was an absolute flyer but I was only at the club for a few months after he joined. From an Exeter perspective Stuart Storer is very unlucky to miss out and would do a good job, but I've got to go for John Hodge.

I've known John since my United days when he came on trial for a while and he was a direct, quick winger who wasn't the biggest of players but had plenty of tricks up his sleeve. We shared digs at Exeter and often used to play golf together at Fingle Glen with Kev Miller, Coops and Jon Brown.

He was daft as a brush at times and one of those characters who got a lot of banter but he could take it, to be fair. He was the leading scorer and appearance-maker in 1992/93 and one of those players you enjoyed playing alongside.

There's footage on YouTube of him doing a forward roll after scoring against Plymouth Argyle, and his form earned him a transfer to Swansea City, before enjoying spells at Walsall, Gillingham and Northampton Town.

Centre midfield – Bryan Robson

I could easily have picked Danny Bailey, who was an absolute warrior and someone I loved playing with. 'You tee him up Dan and I'll smash him!' As well as Danny, there was Russ Coughlin, Eamonn Collins and Steve Williams at Exeter, who were all quality players.

However, I simply have to go with my hero, Bryan Robson. He was the complete footballer and has god-like status at Manchester United. To get the opportunity to play alongside him a couple of times when he was coming back from injury was one of the biggest thrills of my life.

Robbo could do everything and was the ultimate midfield player. He was a warrior and if his game had a weakness it was probably being too brave for his own good. He's sometimes compared to Roy Keane when fans are debating United's greatest-ever captain. Not much separates them but I think what gives Robbo the edge in my humble opinion is he scored the type of goals that Keano couldn't. If you look back at his career he scored some absolute crackers.

He carried United for years and I was pleased that he picked up a couple of Premier League titles towards the end of his career. He had an aura about him that still remains. I attended an executive dinner a while ago where he was one of the guest speakers, and even then all the fans were following him around all night. Simply the best!

Centre midfield – Alan Tonge

The manager's blind spot! 'Just hold the middle of the pitch today, Tongey, and let Robbo do your running for you.' Maybe in a parallel universe. I couldn't miss the opportunity to play alongside these lads again, though.

Solid but unspectacular is probably how I'd describe myself. I like to think I was an unselfish player and reliable team-mate who excelled in winning the ball back and giving it to others, or doing man-marking jobs. I could apply myself and liked to get stuck in because I hated losing.

I wasn't going to beat two or three players but I was a decent passer who could play a nice ball in behind or out wide. Honest, maybe too honest as daft as it sounds and, given my career was cut short at the age of 22, there'll always be a question around it that, sadly, I'll never be able to answer, although I'm proud of what I did achieve.

Make no mistake, I'm doing Robbo's donkey work.

Left wing – Ryan Giggs

The likes of Lee Sharpe, Jules Maiorana and Martin Phillips could all stake a claim here but they're not getting in ahead of Giggsy.

Ryan was an unbelievable player who was tipped for stardom from a very young age. He was a brilliant dribbler of the ball with plenty of pace and tricks to give defenders problems. You could maybe say the one weakness in his game was that he didn't have much of a right foot but, to be fair, he didn't need it because he could still cut inside or put a good cross in.

He was also a very intelligent player and even in his later years when his pace had deteriorated he became an effective squad player who played until he was 40. When debating United's greatest-ever player he's definitely in the discussion, given his longevity and the number of trophies he won.

It was a pleasure to play alongside him as a youngster in the youth teams and watch him develop into a superstar.

Centre-forward – Mark Hughes

Honourable mentions to the likes of Brian McClair, Mark Robins, Shaun Goater, Eamonn Dolan, Ronnie Jepson and Stevie Moran here, but I've got to go with Sparky and Big Norm up top.

I played alongside Mark Hughes in the Histon friendly and he was another player that I'd grown up watching, so it was a privilege. I remember my dad taking me to Burnden Park to watch United's youth team play Bolton in the Lancashire Youth Cup when I was about ten. United won 4-2 and my dad still remembers Sparky standing out as a good prospect. That team actually got to the FA Youth Cup Final in 1982 but were beaten over two legs by a Watford team that included John Barnes.

Sparky was very quiet off the pitch but on it he was an absolute warrior, a strong lad who was very good at using his body to shield the ball and wrestle with defenders. He wasn't the biggest but he was compact with a nasty streak in him. Great touch, good in the air and could score goals. As a centre-forward he was instrumental in United's early success under Fergie and had a top career before moving into management.

If I could bottle the feeling I had when I clipped a ball into his feet at Histon and he shouted 'great ball!' I'd live a fantastic life.

Centre-forward – Norman Whiteside

Norman was another player I idolised as a youngster and I have fond memories of him scoring absolute crackers in both the 1983 FA Cup semi-final versus Arsenal at Villa Park and the 1985 FA Cup Final against Everton at Wembley. He said to me once that the latter was a goal made at The Cliff from hours of practising. It was so intelligent the way he weighed up the situation and curled the ball around the defender Pat van den Hauwe and past Neville Southall into the bottom corner. Absolute class!

He was only 16 when he burst on to the scene and he still holds the record as the youngest player to play in a World Cup, which he achieved for Northern Ireland in 1982. He developed physically very early, which was demonstrated by his goal in the Milk Cup Final in 1983 when he turned Alan Hansen. He was as hard as nails and could put it about if he needed to, as Steve McMahon will testify.

I was fortunate to play alongside and also against him at reserve-team level. He was one of those players who always seemed to be two or three steps ahead, always with time and space, bringing the ball down before flicking it out to the wing.

Honestly, the guy was so good he could have found space in a phone box.

Norman peaked early in his career and, like me, had to retire young through injury. By the time I arrived at United as an apprentice, injuries had taken their toll on him but he always made time for us, having come through the youth ranks himself. He was a character who liked a pint but was also very grounded.

He was also kind enough to write the foreword for this book, for which I'm very grateful – legend!

Chapter 23

Recollections

Mike Pollitt

I first met Alan in the early 1980s while playing for a local team called Moss Bank. He was a box-to-box midfielder who always stood out because he had the ability to score goals from 25 or 30 yards with pace and accuracy, which was very unusual for a lad in his early teens. You could tell from an early age he was a gifted footballer who had a great chance of making it.

We kind of went on the same footballing journey, playing for Bolton town team together while going from club to club on trial, then moving on to Bolton Lads Club at the age of about 14 where things started to get more serious for us under Tony Moulden and Billy Howarth.

They brought a strong discipline and training regime used at many professional football clubs. Tony's son Paul was at Manchester City, while Billy's son Lee was at Blackpool, so they knew what it took and the levels of dedication and professionalism required. Four of us – Alan, myself, Paul Sixsmith and Jason Lydiate – went on to sign for Manchester United together as apprentices. It was quite an achievement for one Sunday league team in Bolton to have so many players sign for such a famous club.

We started training full-time with United on leaving school, catching the bus to The Cliff in Salford before having breakfast every morning with the most successful manager in Manchester United history, Alex Ferguson, who was first in and last out every day.

We just took it for granted but it's fantastic when you look back at it now.

Alan and I played together in the 'A' and 'B' teams in the Lancashire League as it was back then, which was a great education where we'd often find ourselves playing against men. We'd also play friendly matches against the likes of Rochdale, Chester and Bury to help toughen us up, and I'm sure Alan would agree it was sink or swim.

Dressing rooms were brutal places in those days too, and it was a tough environment to grow up in. I must say it taught me how to behave further on in my career and about respect and discipline, because if you stepped out of line our youth-team coach Eric Harrison, who was one of the hardest, toughest but fairest men, would come down on you like a ton of bricks!

In the afternoon after training we all had jobs to do: cleaning boots, putting kits away, sweeping the dressing rooms – you name it, we did it. Alan, Paul and I were always keen to leave so we could get the two buses back to Bolton, but you knew if the manager or Archie Knox came down to the dressing room for a sauna that we weren't going home early! One finger of dust and that was it, we'd have to get changed again and start cleaning. Many a time we got home at some godforsaken hour. It's only when you look back now that you realise why they did it: it was to keep you grounded and humble so you didn't think you'd made it as a player at Manchester United.

We had some great times there, winning most competitions we played in, with some fantastic runs in the FA Youth Cup and travelling to numerous different countries. I wouldn't swap any of it for the world and I'm sure Alan will agree.

We were all rewarded with professional contracts and I know Alan played quite a few matches in the reserves, having been converted to a right-back. It was more difficult for me, being a goalkeeper, so I moved on after a year to try to forge a career, and luckily I'm still in football to this day.

Alan's journey was a little different after leaving United. He went down to Exeter City, where he played under Alan Ball in their first team before a serious injury forced him to retire at a young age, which must have been very traumatic. To his absolute credit he's managed to get over the disappointment of losing his football dream and retrain himself as a university lecturer. I think telling people his story will hopefully inspire others to realise that when one door shuts another opens.

It's great to see him these days keeping close to his footballing roots by being an active member of the Manchester United former players' association and commentating on Exeter City's away matches. I have nothing but fond words to say about Alan and his family, who are probably the nicest people I've met on my own footballing journey.

Kieran Toal

I first came across Alan when we were hopeful schoolboys training twice a week at The Cliff with Eric Harrison, on Monday and Thursday evenings. Alan was part of a quintet of Bolton-based schoolboys who were all highly rated, and Fergie made it clear when he signed those lads that he was intent on 'going local'. It was certainly a strategy he was committed to and one that had a positive impact on me as another local lad signed by the club at Easter 1987.

Alan was a talented right-back and occasional centre-half. We always got on and I can't ever remember a cross word between us. He was matter-of-fact, committed, and expected the same of his team-mates. He also had a strong and supportive family behind him. I remember his dad and brother were devoted followers of Alan's career, as you would expect, watching most if not all of his matches.

One of the things I remember vividly about Alan was that while initially he was a good, solid defender who was a competitor and difficult to get the better of, he wasn't overly aggressive. However, that changed under the coaching of Eric Harrison. Eric was tough and demanding. As a former defender himself he wanted his players to be aggressive, and after many months it was like a switch had been flicked in Alan's head – like he'd been eating what Stuart Pearce was having for breakfast! I think Alan realised that to make a career in the game he needed to become nastier – a 'bastard' even. So from being a player who never seemed to pick up bookings he started to collect yellow cards for fun!

Like for many of us, leaving United was clearly a blow for Alan, but I'm delighted with how he used the disappointment and that of his career being cut short by injury to fuel his post-football life. While I think we can all acknowledge that being a young footballer at United in those days was a fantastic experience, it was also a harsh and at times ruthless environment. I like to think the lads who got to experience what we did were better for it and equipped with some of the core skills that help former players survive and thrive outside of football.

Simon Andrews

I've been lucky to be both a team-mate and more recently a close friend of Tongey. As a player he was solid, reliable and dependable, before taking a lot of these attributes into his personal life and career.

He's the type of guy that if he says he's going to do something he does it to the best of his ability. We also share a love of Manchester United and frequently exchange messages about players and the current goings-on at the club.

In a world full of blaggers and charlatans, Tongey is the opposite. A great, well-meaning guy with strong values and principles.

Craig Lawton

Well, Alan certainly left an impression on me during our time coming through the ranks at Manchester United. And by that I mean I often caught his flying studs on my shins and picked up a few colourful bruises from some strong and robust tackles.

With Tongey being a right-back and me being a left-winger our paths crossed in many a training session at The Cliff or Littleton Road under the watchful eye of Eric Harrison. He was the perfect conduit for Eric's rough, tough and no-nonsense approach. Eric would be barking orders, which Tongey was more than happy to carry out, right down to the finest detail – even if it meant stopping his opponent by any means with one-footed scything tackles, sometimes two! It was always with the intention of taking the ball first, although on a few occasions it came second! I always thought Eric had a soft spot for Tongey and maybe he saw a bit of himself in him as a young lad, with a ferocious appetite for the game.

I remember one training drill we used to do in the small gym at The Cliff called 2v2. We'd have the whole gym with a small bench at either end as a goal, then you'd have four young lads full of testosterone battling it out and anything would go for a few minutes. There would be tackles flying in, elbows being used, shoulders, knees – you name it. Needless to say this was one of Tongey's favourite sessions in which he excelled. As you can imagine, he caused many a scuffle and punches to be thrown before the coaches intervened to calm things down.

Tongey was a hard, tough-tackling, no-nonsense, enthusiastic and determined footballer who gave 120 per cent every time he stepped over the line. Off the pitch he was one of the nicest lads you could meet and always had a smile on his face. He genuinely loved the game, the rapport with the coaches and the banter with the lads in the dressing room.

Paul McGuinness

Alan, I remember we played together in the reserves and 'A' team at United. The boss had got me back after I'd been at Loughborough University as the reserve team had struggled and nearly got relegated from the Central League. Lads like Russell Beardsmore, Tony Gill, David Wilson, Deiniol Graham and Lee Martin had been pushed up to the first team and the manager wanted to fill that experience gap.

I think you'd have been youth-team age or just a bit older and I remember, of course, that strong, deep voice and accent, which gave away how you were going to play – tough, no-nonsense, always hard to beat and enthusiastic.

Alan, I always got the feeling you were fully in love with the idea of being a United youth-team player and the importance of following in the footsteps of the great players who had gone before. Settling for nothing less than giving your all as a 'guardian' of that spirit of United. I felt it ran through my veins and I could tell those who felt the same and those that didn't.

Ryan Giggs – speaking to a podcast in 2016

Alan was a good player, similar to Lee Dixon really, who knew the position (playing at right-back). It was always tough training against him because he was an intelligent player.

Kevin Miller

I recall meeting Tongey for the first time and his accent being so strong I couldn't understand what he was saying. His favourite phrase was, 'Alrrrrrright?'

Tongey kept himself to himself and just went about his business as a very steady player with a very dry sense of humour. Him and Coops were inseparable in the house where we all lived in digs together on Pennsylvania Road, and we shared many a night out, which would never happen these days.

After I moved clubs we lost contact but we all got back together at the end of the Covid pandemic and played in a charity match at Tiverton Town. Tongey still hadn't changed, neither had his walk, favourite phrase and sense of humour.

What a great lad, and I often see him at our away fixtures up north where he does the radio commentary (there's a line I could use here, Tongey, but I won't).

To sum Tongey up in two words – top guy.

Jon Brown

My recollection of Alan: your stereotypical Manc, a salt-of-the-earth man and a good honest pro who would go into battle for the cause. I first met Alan when he came from Manchester United to

Exeter City as a young pro in the early 90s and he really fitted in with all the boys with his down-to-earth, no-nonsense approach.

Whatever role he was given within the team, he dealt with it in a straightforward and professional manner, always giving 100 per cent commitment, including man-marking jobs – just ask Warren Joyce! And he could play. A great team-mate.

Danny Bailey

My experiences with my warrior, team-mate and brother, Alan Tonge …

As one of the senior professionals at Exeter City, I had the honour of lining up alongside a young and uncompromising Alan Tonge in the 1992/93 season under the guidance and leadership of Alan Ball. Our job was breaking down opposition attacks, while creating our own opportunities.

Having Alan in the team was like having your twin brother play alongside you. The same qualities I had, I saw in Alan. He had the will to win, never gave up and always fought to the end. All of these qualities, he possesses through to the present day.

Jon Richardson

I had the pleasure of being Tongey's boot boy during my time as an apprentice at Exeter City. He was an excellent professional on and off the pitch and helped me out a lot as a young player, giving plenty of advice.

I remember one year that Christmas was coming up and all the apprentices were banking on getting a nice tip off the pros for doing their boots; however, before that we had to sing a song in front of the first-team lads in our birthday suits. I remember singing 'Jingle Bells' and getting showered in tea, water, biscuits and whatever else was being thrown at us. Good times (I think). Afterwards Tongey didn't disappoint and gave me a decent tip, which made the whole experience worthwhile.

Joking aside, it was an absolute pleasure to play alongside Tongey and have him as a team-mate and a friend.

Cheers. Tongey. Top man.

Gary Rice

I had the pleasure of meeting and playing alongside Alan at Exeter City in the mid-1990s when I was an apprentice who cleaned his boots. Although he didn't tip very well!!!

He'd spend time with the apprentices, giving us the benefit of his experience and advice, which was welcomed as you didn't always get it from the senior pros. It shows the type of character and team player he was.

We all felt for him when he had to retire due to injury and I for one am proud of what he has gone on to achieve in the academic arena and on a personal level. Only joking about the tips!

John Hodge

My first memory of Alan was at Man United when I came down on trial in the late 80s. He was an apprentice at the time and I can remember training and playing with him.

Our paths crossed again a few years later when he came to Exeter City. I was already at the club and we ended up rooming together in digs. We became good friends and spent quite a bit of time together outside of football, sometimes knocking a ball about in the afternoons or golfing at a place called Fingle Glen.

Alan would give me a lift to training in his red Ford Orion and I remember he used to have The Beatles on a lot, including the track 'A Day in the Life'. When we used to roll up, the other lads often gave us pelters and would ask what the hell was blaring out!

As a footballer, Alan was solid as a rock and never let you down. He always gave 100 per cent and if the ball went past him the attacker certainly didn't! He was no-nonsense and an absolute monster at times, regularly finding his way into the referee's notebook. It wasn't always about rough and tumble though, as Alan could play too. He always kept it simple and rarely gave the ball away.

I think Alan Ball, who was the manager of Exeter City at the time, saw quite a bit of himself in Alan. They were both from a similar area up north and had suffered the experience of being released while young players. It came across in their relationship.

Alan kept himself to himself and didn't really say too much but was very well-respected in the dressing room. It was devastating that he had to retire at such a young age but I'm glad he eventually managed to find another worthwhile career path and do some really good things from an educational perspective.

Football can be cruel and unforgiving at times. It's a short career and at some stage we all have to find something else to do – some earlier than others.

Dave Cooper

I first met Alan when he arrived at digs in Exeter in the early 90s. We'd both been at top division clubs in Manchester United and Luton Town, respectively, so had something in common straight away. After suffering a previous knock-back, we were two young lads trying to move on with our careers.

From day one we got on exceptionally well and spent a lot of time together across the two or three different digs we stayed at.

We ended up rooming together and I must say Alan was one of the worst snorers ever. I used to keep rolled-up socks at the side of my bed, and I'd throw them at him to wake him up!

We'd often play golf, have a few pints or punts in the bookies after training. Alan Ball used to know the racehorse trainer Mick Channon so would regularly pass us tips; it was a different culture back then.

As players we also had a lot in common. I loved the tackling side of the game and so did Alan, with Bally using us both in man-marking roles. He identified danger men in the opposition team and got us to follow them all over the place, smashing into them when we could. We carried out those orders to a tee many times but could play football when the opportunity arose, so had a nice combination of qualities.

Tragically, we both had to retire very young due to serious injuries, myself with a bad leg break and Alan with a spinal problem. We helped each other through those tough times as we had to partake in long, intense rehab programmes to try to get back to a professional level of fitness. I've kept in touch with Alan over the years and will always consider him to be a good mate and top man. We still laugh about the old times and always come to the same conclusion. It's a good job there weren't any camera phones or recording equipment back then!

After the gut-wrenching experience of us both having to come out of professional football at a relatively tender age, it's great to see Alan has moved on with his life into a successful teaching career. He's even managed to achieve a PhD – wow! That's incredible really. There aren't many former professional footballers, especially from Manchester United, who can say they've got one of those.

Dr Mark Nesti – Sports Psychologist

To make a career in the game as a professional footballer always requires certain psychological skills and qualities. Some of these are related to the ability to make the right decision under pressure but others are deeper than this and are more about passion and motivation for the game itself. Psychologists talk about intrinsic motivation; that is, in more ordinary language, the deep love that someone has to possess to do something purely for its own sake. I know through the many years of working in Premier League football at first-team level with players from across the world who have come through the academy that most of these individuals, among other psychological qualities, are highly intrinsically motivated and possess considerable levels of self-belief. What's rarely understood and most certainly comes as a shock to most parents and young people who try to enter the profession is how few will make the progression from youth-team levels into full-time first-team professional football at any level.

This journey requires effort, huge resilience and persistence, self-belief and deep levels of motivation. It also requires a very large slice of luck. The result of this is that players often don't progress from youth levels and are discarded by clubs for one reason or another, and this also happens to those lucky few who do have professional careers.

I know in the case of Alan that he did make the transition through into senior professional football and this brought him a wonderful experience and deep disappointment at being signed by Manchester United then released by the club after a relatively short period of time. The journey, though, is still fraught, despite the exciting and wonderful moments, because in his case he experienced an injury that was chronic and severe and eventually forced him to leave the game prematurely. At this juncture, Alan, like so many others schooled in the traditional British working-class culture where formal academic qualifications and high-level education have so often been seen as the preserve of the middle class, found himself with few qualifications and a dream crushed.

It's at these critical moments that somebody will question exactly who they are. These are moments of existential crisis around identity and, for some, without the right level of support, whether that be from family or other skilled professionals, despair, depression, anxiety and even worse can emerge and take hold. In Alan's case the story has a much better trajectory. He managed to find his way on to a degree programme that allied his love of science, psychology and football, which challenged him to collect the educational attainments but more importantly the knowledge and ability to think critically that maybe he hadn't developed earlier in his life. Beyond this he then eventually pursued a PhD in his own area of psychology applied to football. This is something that we'd like to see more and more young athletes pursue, but especially in sports like football where there has often been for so long suspicion and even derision about the value of formal academic qualifications.

Alan now sits in a very special place in terms of his life and career where he's able to draw on a lived experience in the game of professional football and yet be fully aware of the need for self-development, self-knowledge and educational attainment. Not only can these matters be useful at the end of a career, no matter how long or short this may be, but it's increasingly recognised that pursuing other valuable interests outside of the game can develop a more rounded player, someone with greater resilience and an individual with more perspective in terms of the difficulties and challenges that they may face. The intensity that's required of professional players is as it should be, given that very few are operating at this level of excellence. Nevertheless, there's a great need to develop, holistically, a much more balanced and rounded identity. After all, although football is a wonderful dream of so many young people and others, eventually the dream ends and a new life must be faced and embraced.

Dr Rob Morris – Sports Psychologist

The challenges that athletes like Alan face when transitioning away from a sport they've dedicated their lives to are immense and often underestimated. The sudden shift from a highly structured and adrenaline-filled environment to a more conventional setting can be a shock to one's identity and mental well-being. The camaraderie, the sense of purpose, the daily rhythm of training and competition that define an athlete's life can be difficult to replace.

Alan's story emphasises the importance of finding new passions, like education in Alan's case, to fill that void and provide a fresh sense of purpose. Alan's journey from a professional football career to retraining, pursuing higher education and eventually achieving a PhD is a testament to the power of determination and the capacity to overcome challenges. It highlights that life is a continuous evolution, where the skills and qualities cultivated in sport can be seamlessly transferred to other domains. Alan's story serves as an inspiration not only to athletes but to anyone facing major life transitions. I applaud Alan's courage in sharing such a personal and impactful journey, and I have no doubt that this book will resonate with readers on various levels.

Lauren Tonge-Ward

When I think of my dad, it's hard to picture the illustrious career and life he lived pre-children. To me, he's just the guy that gives me lifts and secretly bungs me £20 every now and then!

It was only when he asked me to put a few words on to paper that I truly comprehended the extent of what he achieved professionally, especially considering that he was the age that I am now. However, what strikes me the most isn't the number of appearances, the clubs he played for, the trophies he won or the countries he travelled to. Instead, what strikes me the most, as his daughter, is the power of mind he must have commandeered when his whole world fell apart.

Finally living out his childhood dream, he stood facing a turn of events that no young man should ever have to experience. But growing up in the wake of those events he showed me that, day after day, you must always wake up and choose life, no matter the hurdles. He showed me that nothing is impossible if you work hard enough and I don't think I could be prouder to call him my dad.

Sam Tonge

I'm immensely proud of my dad's achievements both during and after his football career. To go through the ranks and achieve a professional contract at one of the biggest football clubs in the world is an outstanding achievement and something that has inspired me massively in my life.

Furthermore, the way my dad has bounced back from his football career ending is truly inspirational. To pick himself back up and re-engage with his education then become a lecturer in sports psychology and complete a PhD is remarkable. He's one of a kind.

Dr Alan Tonge – Career Stats

Manchester United 1986–91
'B' team – 41 appearances, 0 goals
'A' team – 55 appearances, 0 goals
Reserves – 13 appearances, 0 goals
FA Youth Cup – 10 appearances, 0 goals
First-team friendly – 19 May 1989 at Abbey Stadium, Cambridge;
Histon 1-3 Manchester United XI; substitute for Lee Martin
Total appearances including friendlies – 168

Achievements:
1988/89
Lancashire League Division Two winner
FA Youth Cup – quarter-finals

1989/90
Grossi-Morera tournament winner
Lancashire League Division One winner
FA Youth Cup – semi-finals
Lancashire FA Youth Cup – semi-finals

1990/91
Lancashire League Division One winner
Blue Stars Zurich tournament runner-up

Horwich RMI – 1991

Exeter City – 1991–94
First team – 27 appearances, 2 goals
Devon and Exeter Premier League winner – 1991/92 and 1992/93
Autoglass Trophy regional finalist – 1992/93
Exeter City young player of the year award – 1992/93

Elmore – 1994–95

Clyst Rovers – 1995–96

Academic Qualifications
BSc in Sports Science and Leisure – 2003
PGCE in Further, Wider and Higher Education – 2004
MPhil (Master of Philosophy) – 2010
DPhil (Doctor of Philosophy) – 2022

90 0790242 8